Insights
for Today

Fourth Edition

Reading for Today SERIES, BOOK 2

D0128284

LORRAINE C. SMITH

AND

NANCY NICI MARE

English Language Institute
Queens College
The City University of New York

HEINLE
CENGAGE Learning

Australia • Brazil • Japan • Korea • Mexico • Singapore • Spain • United Kingdom • United States

HEINLE
CENGAGE Learning·

Reading for Today 2: Insights for Today, Fourth Edition
Lorraine C. Smith and Nancy Nici Mare

Publisher, the Americas, Global, and Dictionaries: Sherrise Roehr

Acquisitions Editor: Thomas Jefferies

Senior Development Editor:
Laura Le Dréan

Senior Content Project Manager:
Maryellen Killeen

Director of US Marketing:
James McDonough

Senior Product Marketing Manager:
Katie Kelley

Academic Marketing Manager:
Caitlin Driscoll

Director of Global Marketing: Ian Martin

Senior Print Buyer: Betsy Donaghey

Compositor: Pre-PressPMG

Cover and Interior Design: Muse Group

Printer: RR Donnelley

Library of Congress Control Number: 2010922336

ISBN–13: 978-1-111-03361-3

ISBN–10: 1-111-03361-7

Heinle
20 Channel Center Street
Boston, MA 02210
USA

Cengage Learning is a leading provider of customized learning solutions with office locations around the globe, including Singapore, the United Kingdom, Australia, Mexico, Brazil, and Japan. Locate your local office at: **international.cengage.com/region**

Cengage Learning products are represented in Canada by Nelson Education, Ltd.

For your course and learning solutions, visit **academic.cengage.com**

Purchase any of our products at your local college store or at our preferred online store **www.CengageBrain.com**

Printed in the United States of America
1 2 3 4 5 6 7 14 13 12 11 10

CREDITS

CONTENTS

Skills Chart ix

Preface xiii

Introduction xvi

Acknowledgments xxiii

UNIT 1 Today's Travelers 1

Chapter 1   **A Family Sees America Together** 2
An American family travels across the country in a van. They want to see all 50 states and meet the different people of the United States.

Courtney's Texas—Big History, Big Cities, Big Hearts 12
The daughter of the family writes in her journal every day. She describes the places and the people. Today, she writes about Texas.

Chapter 2   **Volunteer Vacations** 20
Many people like to take a vacation to relax. But some people use their vacations to do something different: they do volunteer work to help others.

Who Volunteers? 31
Many different kinds of people are volunteers. Some are young college graduates; others are senior citizens. But they all enjoy the work!

UNIT 2 Family Life 39

Chapter 3   **How Alike Are Identical Twins?** 40
Identical twins are not very common. Scientists study them to understand their differences and similarities.

Diary of a Triplet Father 54
This father has triplets! In his diary, he describes his busy life with his three children.

Chapter 4   **The Search for Happiness through Adoption**   **62**

People adopt children for different reasons. However, they all love their adopted children and want a happy life together.

Diary of an Adoptive Mother   **77**

A woman is adopting a child from another country. In her diary she writes about her feelings, her hopes, and her dreams.

UNIT 3

Technology in Our Everyday Lives
    87

Chapter 5   **Robots: The Face of the Future**   **88**

Robots are very useful machines. They can do dangerous or boring work. They can conduct an orchestra. They can even clean your home.

An Unusual Teacher   **101**

In Japan, students in a 6th-grade class have an unusual teacher. Their teacher is not a person. Their teacher is a robot!

Chapter 6   **A New Way To Go**   **108**

New scooters can take you anywhere. They are faster than walking, and they save energy, too.

Young Inventors   **120**

Young people use their imaginations to make new, useful inventions. They can also win money for college at the same time.

UNIT 4

Healthy Living
    129

Chapter 7   **Improving Lives with Pet Therapy**   **130**

Pets give us company and keep us from being lonely, but not everyone knows that pets can help us be healthy. They can even help children read better.

A New Way to Relieve Student Stress   **143**
Before exams, college students study hard, and feel very stressed. A dog companion can help them relax more and worry less.

Chapter 8   **A Healthy Diet for Everyone**   **150**
What food is good for you? Some food can help you stay healthy, but some food can make you sick. Do you know which kinds of food to eat?

Why Do I Eat When I'm Not Hungry?   **165**
Sometimes people eat for other reasons besides hunger. However, there are steps you can take to avoid eating when you're not hungry.

UNIT 5   ## International Scientists   175

Chapter 9   **Alfred Nobel: A Man of Peace**   **176**
The world remembers Alfred Nobel for different reasons. He wanted to be remembered as a peaceful man.

Choosing Nobel Prize Winners   **189**
It is a great honor to win a Nobel Prize. Different groups decide who the winners will be. Nobel Prize winners receive something else, too.

Chapter 10   **Marie Curie: Nobel Prize Winner**   **197**
This great scientist was a very modern woman. She was the first female to receive the Nobel Prize.

Irene Curie   **212**
The daughter of the famous scientists continued her mother's work and also won a Nobel Prize.

UNIT 6 The Earth's Resources and Dangers   221

Chapter 11   **Oil as an Important World Resource**   222
Oil is one of the world's most useful natural resources. People use it in many different ways.

The DO IT Homestead   237
The Collins family of Utah uses only solar energy to live. They run their home and their farm using energy from the sun.

Chapter 12   **How Earthquakes Occur**   246
Earthquakes can be deadly, and scientists cannot predict them. We should understand them and learn how to protect ourselves in an earthquake.

A Survivor's Story   261
An elderly woman who lived through the Kobe, Japan earthquake describes this frightening event.

Index of Key Words and Phrases   273
Skills Index   277

Unit	Chapter and Title	Reading Skills Focus	Structure Focus	Follow-up Activities Skills Focus
Unit 1 **Today's Travelers** *Page 1*	**Chapter 1** **A Family Sees America Together** *Page 2* **Courtney's Texas** *Page 12*	• Preview visuals and use titles and prereading questions to activate prior knowledge • Understand True/False, Multiple Choice, Short Answer questions • Skim reading for main idea • Scan for information • Recall information, make inferences, draw conclusions • Choose accurate dictionary definitions • Use context clues to understand vocabulary • Read and understand maps	• Identify parts of speech in context: nouns and verbs • Use singular and plural nouns • Use the simple present tense	• *Listening-Speaking:* Express opinions • *Writing:* Make a plan; write an opinion paragraph; write a journal entry
	Chapter 2 **Volunteer Vacations** *Page 20* **Who Volunteers?** *Page 31*	• Use graphic organizers to organize answers and activate prior knowledge • Understand True/False, Multiple Choice, Short Answer questions • Skim reading for main idea • Scan for information and use a chart to record ideas • Use context clues to understand vocabulary • Choose accurate dictionary definitions • Make inferences • Give opinions	• Identify parts of speech in context: nouns and verbs • Recognize the suffix: *-tion* • Use singular and plural nouns • Use affirmative or negative forms of the simple present tense	• *Listening-Speaking:* Share information; make a list of interview questions in pairs; listen and share opinions • *Writing:* Write an opinion paragraph with supporting reasons and examples; write a journal entry
Unit 2 **Family Life** *Page 39*	**Chapter 3** **How Alike Are Identical Twins?** *Page 40* **Diary of a Triplet Father** *Page 54*	• Use background knowledge to understand reading • Understand True/False, Multiple Choice, Short Answer questions • Skim reading for main idea • Scan for information • Use a graphic organizer to take notes • Use context clues to understand vocabulary • Make inferences and draw conclusions • Choose accurate dictionary definitions	• Identify parts of speech in context: adjectives and nouns; verbs and nouns • Recognize the suffix: *-ness* • Use affirmative or negative forms of the simple present tense • Use singular or plural nouns	• *Listening-Speaking:* Develop interview questions and conduct an interview • *Writing:* Write a descriptive paragraph; write positive and negative reasons; write a journal entry expressing likes and dislikes
	Chapter 4 **The Search for Happiness through Adoption** *Page 62* **Diary of an Adoptive Mother** *Page 77*	• Preview visuals and answer prereading questions to activate prior knowledge • Understand True/False, Multiple Choice, Short Answer questions • Skim reading for main idea • Scan for information and take notes in a chart • Use context clues to understand vocabulary • Choose accurate dictionary definitions • Make inferences; draw conclusions • Read, understand, and use statistics	• Identify parts of speech in context: nouns and verbs • Recognize the suffix: *-ion* • Use affirmative or negative forms of the simple present tense • Use singular or plural nouns	• *Listening:* Listen and note opinions of others • *Writing:* Write a dialogue; write a letter; write an opinion paragraph; write a journal entry

SKILLS

Unit	Chapter and Title	Reading Skills Focus	Structure Focus	Follow-up Activities Skills Focus
Unit 3 **Technology in Our Everyday Lives** *Page 87*	**Chapter 5** **Robots: The Face of the Future** *Page 88* **An Unusual Teacher** *Page 101*	• Preview photos to activate prior knowledge • Understand True/False, Multiple Choice, Short Answer questions • Skim reading for main idea • Scan for information and write notes in a chart • Use context clues to understand vocabulary • Choose accurate dictionary definitions • Make inferences; draw conclusions • Make predictions • Understand content area vocabulary about *robots*	• Identify parts of speech in context: nouns and verbs • Recognize the suffix: *-ment* • Use singular and plural nouns • Use affirmative or negative forms of the simple present and past tenses	• *Writing*: Write and compare lists; write a journal entry justifying an opinion
	Chapter 6 **A New Way to Go** *Page 108* **Young Inventors** *Page 120*	• Use visuals to make predictions • Understand True/False, Multiple Choice, Short Answer Questions • Skim reading for main idea • Read for supporting details • Scan for information • Use a chart to take notes • Make inferences • Use context clues to understand vocabulary • Choose accurate dictionary definitions • Understand content area vocabulary about *inventions*	• Identify parts of speech in context: nouns and verbs • Recognize the suffix: *-ion* • Use affirmative or negative forms of the simple present tense	• *Listening-Speaking*: Create an invention with a group and report on it with visual aids • *Writing*: Write a descriptive paragraph; write a journal entry about a proposed invention
Unit 4 **Healthy Living** *Page 129*	**Chapter 7** **Improving Lives with Pet Therapy** *Page 130* **A New Way to Relieve Student Stress** *Page 143*	• Preview chapter through photos and prereading questions • Understand True/False, Multiple Choice, Short Answer questions • Skim reading for main idea • Scan for information • Take notes in a chart • Use context clues to understand vocabulary • Choose dictionary definitions • Make inferences • Understand content area vocabulary about *pets* and *health*	• Identify parts of speech in context: nouns vs. verbs; nouns vs. adjectives • Recognize the suffix: *-ful* • Use singular and plural nouns • Use affirmative or negative forms of the simple present tense	• *Listening-Speaking*: Explain the reasons for having a pet • *Writing*: Write about feeling stressed and ways you relieve it; write a journal entry explaining what makes you feel stressed
	Chapter 8 **A Healthy Diet for Everyone** *Page 150* **Why Do I Eat When I'm Not Hungry?** *Page 165*	• Preview photos with prereading questions • Understand True/False, Multiple Choice, Short Answer questions • Skim for main idea • Scan for information • Take notes in a flowchart • Use context clues to understand vocabulary • Choose dictionary definitions • Make inferences • Draw conclusions • Understand content area vocabulary about *nutrition* and *health*	• Identify parts of speech in context: nouns and verbs • Recognize the suffix: *-ment* • Use the affirmative or negative of the simple present tense	• *Writing*: Write a list of ways to stay healthy; write a journal entry

SKILLS

Unit	Chapter and Title	Reading Skills Focus	Structure Focus	Follow-up Activities Skills Focus
Unit 5 **International Scientists** *Page 175*	**Chapter 9** **Alfred Nobel: A Man of Peace** *Page 176* **Choosing Nobel Prize Winners** *Page 189*	• Preview photos with prereading questions • Understand True/False, Multiple Choice, Short Answer questions • Skim for main ideas • Scan for information using a graphic organizer to take notes • Use context clues to understand vocabulary • Make inferences • Draw conclusions • Choose dictionary definitions • Understand content area vocabulary about the *Nobel Peace Prize*	• Identify parts of speech in context: nouns and verbs • Recognize the suffixes: *-ion*, *-ation*, and *-ment* • Use singular and plural nouns • Use affirmative and negative forms of the simple present tense	• *Writing*: Write instructions; write a biography; write a support paper arguing in favor of someone; make a list from research at the library; write a journal entry
	Chapter 10 **Marie Curie: Nobel Prize Winner** *Page 197* **Irene Curie** *Page 212*	• Preview photos with prereading questions • Understand True/False, Multiple Choice, Short Answer questions • Skim for main ideas • Scan for information • Take notes on a timeline and explain notes • Use context clues to understand vocabulary • Make inferences; draw conclusions • Choose dictionary definitions • Understand content area vocabulary about scientific experiments	• Identify parts of speech in context: nouns and adjectives • Recognize the suffixes: *-ance*, *-ence*, or *-ness* • Use singular and plural nouns • Use affirmative and negative forms of the past tense	• *Writing*: Fill out a chart with ideas from a partner discussion; write a descriptive paragraph or explanatory paragraph; write a brief comparison; write a process paragraph; write a biography and/ or autobiography; write a journal entry

SKILLS

Unit	Chapter and Title	Reading Skills Focus	Structure Focus	Follow-up Activities Skills Focus
Unit 6 **The Earth's Resources and Dangers** *Page 221*	**Chapter 11** **Oil as an Important World Resource** *Page 222* **The DO IT Homestead** *Page 237*	• Generate a list to activate background knowledge • Fill out flowchart with information • Understand True/False, Multiple Choice, Short Answer questions • Use a flowchart to take notes • Skim for main idea • Scan for information and use a graphic organizer to take notes • Use context clues to understand vocabulary • Make inferences; draw conclusions • Choose dictionary definitions • Read, understand, and extract information from diagrams, a map, and a table	• Identify parts of speech in context: nouns, verbs, and adjectives • Recognize the suffix: *-tion* • Use singular and plural nouns • Use affirmative and negative forms of the simple present tense	• *Writing*: Fill out a chart with ideas from a partner discussion; write a descriptive paragraph; write a process paragraph; write a journal entry
	Chapter 12 **How Earthquakes Occur** *Page 246* **A Survivor's Story** *Page 261*	• Use the title to understand main idea • Understand True/False, Multiple Choice, Short Answer questions • Use a flowchart to take notes • Skim for main idea • Scan for information and use a graphic organizer to take notes • Use context clues to understand vocabulary • Make inferences; draw conclusions • Choose dictionary definitions • Read and draw information from a diagram, a map, and a table	• Identify parts of speech in context: nouns and verbs • Recognize the suffix: *-ment* • Use singular and plural nouns • Use affirmative and negative verb forms appropriately in sentences	• *Writing*: Write a composition from interview notes; write a list of instructions; write a journal entry describing a real or imaginary experience

• **Index of Key Words and Phrases** *Page 273*
• **Skills Index** *Page 277*

PREFACE

Insights for Today, Fourth Edition is a reading skills text intended for high–beginning English-as-a-second or foreign-language (ESL/EFL) students. The topics in this text are fresh and timely, and the book has a strong global focus.

Insights for Today is one in a series of five reading skills texts. The complete series, *Reading for Today*, has been designed to meet the needs of students from the beginning to the advanced levels and includes the following:

- *Reading for Today 1: Themes for Today*   beginning
- *Reading for Today 2: Insights for Today*   high beginning
- *Reading for Today 3: Issues for Today*   intermediate
- *Reading for Today 4: Concepts for Today*   high intermediate
- *Reading for Today 5: Topics for Today*   advanced

Insights for Today, Fourth Edition provides students with essential practice in the types of reading skills they will need in an academic environment. It requires students not only to read text but also to extract basic information from various kinds of charts, graphs, illustrations, and photographs. Beginning-level students are rarely exposed to this type of reading material. Furthermore, students are given the opportunity to speak and write about their own cultures and compare their experiences with those of students from other countries. The text has real-life activities that give students tasks to complete outside the classroom. These tasks provide students with opportunities to practice reading, writing, speaking, and listening to English in the real world. Thus, all four skills are incorporated into each chapter.

Insights for Today, Fourth Edition has been designed for flexible use by teachers and students. The text consists of six units. Each unit contains two chapters that deal with related topics. At the same time, though, each chapter is entirely separate in content from the other chapter in that unit. This gives the instructor the option of either completing entire units or choosing individual chapters as a focus in class. If the teacher chooses to do both chapters, there are discussion questions at the end of each unit to tie the two related topics together. Furthermore, although the chapters are organized by level of difficulty, the teacher and students may choose to work with the chapters out of order, depending on available time and the interests of the class. The activities and exercises in each chapter have been organized to flow from general comprehension, including main ideas and supporting details, through vocabulary in context, to critical thinking skills. However, the teacher may choose to work on certain exercises in any order, depending on time and on the students' abilities.

The opening illustrations and the prereading preparation before each reading help activate the students' background knowledge of the topic and encourage the students to think about the ideas, facts, and vocabulary that will be presented in the passage. In fact, discussing illustrations in class helps lower-level students visualize what they are going to read about and gives them cues for the new vocabulary they will encounter. The exercises that follow the reading passage are intended to develop and improve reading proficiency, including the ability to learn new vocabulary from context and better comprehend English sentence structure. The activities also give students the opportunity to master useful vocabulary encountered in the articles through partner discussion and group work and lead the students through comprehension of main ideas and specific information.

Lower-level language students need considerable visual reinforcement of ideas and vocabulary. This is why this text has many illustrations. It is also why so many of the follow-up activities enable students to manipulate the information in the text and supplemental information. In fact, the teacher may want the students to complete the charts and lists in the activities on the board.

In any given chapter, much of the vocabulary is repeated throughout the exercises and activities. Experience has shown that low-level students especially need a lot of exposure to the same vocabulary and word forms. Repetition of vocabulary in varied contexts helps students not only understand the new vocabulary better but also helps them remember it.

A student-centered approach will facilitate learning. Wherever possible, students should be actively engaged through pair work or small group work. Except during the actual process of reading, students should be actively engaged in almost all of the activities and exercises with a partner or in a small group. By working with others, students have more opportunities to interact in English. Student group work also allows the teacher to circulate in the classroom and give more individual attention to students than would be possible if the teacher directed most of the class work from the front of the room.

As students work through *Insights for Today*, they will learn and improve reading skills, and develop more confidence in their growing English proficiency skills. At the same time, teachers will be able to observe the students' steady progress toward skillful, independent reading.

New to the Fourth Edition

The fourth edition of *Insights for Today* maintains the effective approach of the third edition with several significant improvements. This enhanced edition takes a more in-depth approach to vocabulary development and application by consistently introducing, practicing, and assessing vocabulary in context, while teaching valuable vocabulary-building skills that are recycled throughout the series.

Vocabulary development is emphasized in several sections. First, new *Vocabulary in Context* sections have been added to every chapter; they teach the vocabulary from the reading along with related words and concepts. Second, the *Word Forms* sections now combine statements into paragraphs to further develop the contextualized approach. Finally, *Word Partnership* boxes have been added from the *Collins COBUILD School Dictionary of American English* to help students to use the language appropriately.

The fourth edition also includes two new chapters with cutting edge topics. "Robots: The Face of the Future" describes the uses of robots at work, in the home, and at school. "Improving Lives with Pet Therapy" demonstrates ways that pets can make us healthier and improve our study habits.

Insights for Today has an enhanced *Prereading Preparation* section, which provides thoughtful, motivating illustrations and activities. The fourth edition includes improved graphics, art, and photos to facilitate students' understanding of the text. For an introduction to academic skills, the *Skimming and Scanning* exercises include a main idea activity as well as outlines, charts, and flowcharts. This design takes into account the different learning and organizational styles of the students. For the development of critical thinking skills, the *Think About It* sections challenge students to apply the topic of the chapter to their own lives and draw conclusions.

All these enhancements to *Insights for Today, Fourth Edition* have been designed to help students to improve their reading skills and to develop their confidence as readers, to reinforce vocabulary, and to encourage interest in the topics. All these skills are intended to prepare students for academic work and the technical world of information.

INTRODUCTION

How to Use This Book

Every chapter in this book consists of the following:

- Prereading Preparation
- Reading Passages
- Fact-Finding Exercise
- Skimming and Scanning Exercise
- Reading Analysis
- Dictionary Skills
- Word Forms
- Vocabulary in Context
- Think About It
- Another Look
- Topics for Discussion and Writing
- Follow-Up Activities
- Word Search
- Crossword Puzzle
- Grammar Cloze Quiz

At the end of each unit there is a *Unit Discussion,* which ties together the related topics in the two chapters for that unit.

The format of each chapter in the book is consistent. Although each chapter can be done entirely in class, some exercises may be assigned for homework. This, of course, depends on the individual teacher's preference, as well as the availability of class time.

Prereading Preparation

The prereading activity is designed to activate students' background knowledge, stimulate their interest, and provide preliminary vocabulary for the passage itself. The importance of prereading preparation should not be underestimated. Studies have shown the positive effect of prereading preparation in motivating students and in enhancing reading comprehension. In fact, prereading discussion in general and discussion of visuals have been shown to be very effective in improving reading comprehension. Students need to spend time describing and discussing the illustrations and the prereading questions. Furthermore, students should try to relate the topic to their own experience, and try to predict what they are going to read about. The teacher can facilitate the students' discussions by writing their guesses and predictions about the reading on the board. This procedure helps motivate students by providing a reason for reading. This process also helps the teacher evaluate the students' knowledge of the content they are about to read so she can provide additional background information where needed. After they have read the passage, students can check their predictions for accuracy. The important point to keep in mind is not whether the students' guesses are correct, but rather that they think about the reading beforehand and formulate predictions about the text. Once students have considered the title, the accompanying illustrations, and the prereading questions, they are ready to read the passage.

The Reading Passage

As students read the passage for the first time, they should be encouraged to read *ideas*. After students read the passage to themselves, the teacher may want to read the passage aloud to them. At lower levels, students are very eager to learn pronunciation and feel that this practice is helpful to them. Moreover, reading aloud provides students with an appropriate model for pronunciation and intonation, and helps them hear how words are grouped together by meaning. Students can also listen to the readings on the Audio CD.

Students may wish to maintain individual records of their reading rate. They can keep track of the time it takes them to read a passage for the first time, and then record the length of time it takes them to read it a second time. Students should be encouraged to read a text from beginning to end without stopping, and to read at a steady pace, reading words in meaningful groups or phrases. Once they have established a base time for reading, they can work to improve their reading rate as they progress through the book.

Fact-Finding Exercise

After the first reading, students will have a general idea of the information in the passage. The purpose of the *Fact-Finding Exercise* is to check students' general comprehension. Students will read the *True/False* statements and check whether the information is true or false. If the statement is false, the students will go back to the passage and find the line(s) that contain the correct information. They will then rewrite the statement so that it becomes true. This activity can be done individually or in pairs. Doing this exercise in pairs allows students to discuss their answers with their partner, and to explain their reasons for deciding if a statement is true or false. When all the students have finished the exercise, they can report their answers to the class.

Skimming and Scanning Exercise

Students need to practice two important skills: skimming a reading for the main idea, and scanning it for specific information. Before doing this exercise, the teacher should point out to the students the difference in purpose between skimming and scanning, and explain that each activity requires a different way to read. When skimming, it is helpful for the students to keep the title in mind, and to ask themselves, "What is this reading telling me about?" In the first part of the activity, students are asked to read the passage a second time in order to understand the main idea of the reading. When preparing students for this exercise, the teacher should encourage them to ignore unknown vocabulary and to focus on understanding the most important idea of the reading. When going over the exercise, the teacher should discuss with the students why the other answers are incorrect. In the second part of the activity, students should be instructed to scan the passage carefully again and to pay attention to details. They will complete a chart or an outline, or answer questions on specific information in the passage, and compare their answers with a classmate's. The pairs of students can then refer back to the passage and check their answers. When the class is finished, one or more students can complete the chart or outline on the board so students can check and discuss their answers as a class.

Reading Analysis

At this point, students have read the passage at least three times, and should be familiar with the main idea and the content of the reading. The *Reading Analysis* exercise gives students an opportunity to learn new vocabulary from context. In this exercise students read questions and answer them. This exercise requires students to think about the meanings of words and phrases, the structure of sentences and paragraphs, and the relationships of ideas to each other. This exercise is very effective when done in pairs or in groups. Students can also work individually, but working together is an excellent opportunity for students to discuss possible answers.

Dictionary Skills

The entries in this section have been taken from Heinle's *Newbury House Dictionary of American English*. This exercise provides students practice with using an English-English dictionary, while teaching them the appropriate and relevant meanings of unfamiliar words. Students are given dictionary entries for words from the reading passage. A sentence containing the unknown word is provided below each entry. Students read the entry and select the appropriate definition, given the context provided. Students need to understand that this is not always a clear process; some entries are similar. They should be encouraged to read carefully all of the possible definitions in the context in which the word is given, and to consider which meaning makes the most sense. After selecting the appropriate entry, students read two or three sentences and choose which one conveys the meaning of the definition selected. Students can work in pairs on this exercise and report back to the class. They should be prepared to justify their choice.

Word Forms

As an introduction to the *Word Forms* exercises in this book, it is recommended that teachers first review parts of speech, especially verbs, nouns, adjectives, and adverbs. Teachers should point out the position of each word form in a sentence. Students will develop a sense for which part of speech is missing in a given sentence. Teachers should also point out clues to tense and number, and whether an idea is affirmative or negative. Each section has its own instructions, depending on the particular pattern that is being introduced. For example, in the section containing words that take *-tion* in the noun form, teachers can explain that in this exercise students will look at the verb and noun forms of two types of words that use the suffix *-tion* in their noun form. (1) Some words simply add *-tion* to the verb: suggest/suggestion; if the word ends in *e*, the *e* is dropped first: produce/production; (2) other words can drop the final *e* and add *-ation:* examine/examination. Teachers can use the examples in the directions for each chapter's *Word Forms* section and in the *Word Partnership* box at the end of each section to see that the students understand the exercise. This activity is very effective when done in pairs because students can discuss their answers. After students have a working knowledge of this type of exercise, it can be assigned for homework. The *Word Partnership* box at the end of this section is selected from the *Collins COBUILD School Dictionary of American English.* The words in these boxes are used to reinforce the vocabulary that appears in the readings.

Vocabulary in Context

This is a fill-in exercise designed as a review of the vocabulary items covered in the *Reading Analysis, Dictionary Skills,* or *Word Forms* exercises. It can be assigned for homework as a review or done in class as group work.

Think About It

The goal of this exercise is for students to go beyond the reading itself and to form their own ideas and opinions on aspects of the topic. Students should reflect on the content of the reading and think about the implications of the information they have read. Students can work on these questions as an individual writing exercise or orally as a small-group discussion activity. In this activity, students are encouraged to use the vocabulary they have learned.

Another Look

The second reading in each chapter provides another point of view, or an additional topic, related to the main reading. Students should focus on general comprehension, on relating this reading to the primary reading, and on considering the ideas and information as they engage in the *Follow-Up Activities* and *Topics for Discussion and Writing.* It is not necessary to spend additional time on unfamiliar vocabulary, unless it interferes with students' ability to respond to the questions.

Topics for Discussion and Writing

This section provides ideas or questions for the students to think about and work on alone, in pairs, or in small groups. Students are encouraged to use the information and vocabulary from the passages both orally and in their writing. The writing assignments may be done entirely in class, begun in class and finished at home, or done at home. The last activity in this section is a journal-writing assignment that provides students with an opportunity to reflect on the topic in the chapter and respond to it in some personal way. Students should be encouraged to keep a journal and to write in it regularly. The students' journal writing may be purely personal, or students may choose to have the teacher read their entries. If the teacher reads the entries, the journals should be considered a free writing activity, and should be responded to rather than corrected.

Follow-Up Activities

This section contains various activities appropriate to the information in the passages. Some activities are designed for pair and small group work. Students are encouraged to use the information and vocabulary from the passages both orally and in writing. Teachers may also use these questions and activities as homework or in-class assignments. The *Follow-Up Activities* help students interact with the real world because many exercises require students to go outside the classroom to collect specific information. Students are not limited to speaking, reading, or learning in the classroom only.

Word Search

Doing the *Word Search* exercise gives students an opportunity to practice recognizing words. This activity contains several words from the main reading. The words appear in every direction: left to right, right to left, top to bottom, bottom to top, and diagonally. It may be done individually first, and then students can compare their work. Students often enjoy this type of word puzzle because it is challenging, yet not too difficult. Even weaker students experience success with this type of word puzzle. Students can complete the *Word Search* activity on their own or with a partner after they have completed another in-class assignment and are waiting for the rest of their classmates to finish their work.

Crossword Puzzle

The *Crossword Puzzle* in each chapter is based on the vocabulary used in that chapter. Students can go over the puzzle orally if pronunciation practice with letters is needed. Teachers can have the students spell out their answers in addition to pronouncing the word itself. Students invariably enjoy doing crossword puzzles. They are a fun way to reinforce the vocabulary presented in the various exercises in each chapter. Puzzles also require students to pay attention to correct spelling. At the same time, students need to connect the meaning of a word and think of the word itself. If the teacher prefers, students can do the Crossword Puzzle on their own or with a partner in their free time, or after they have completed an in-class assignment and are waiting for the rest of their classmates to finish.

Grammar Cloze Quiz

The *Grammar Cloze Quiz* exercise in each chapter serves as a final review of the primary reading. These quizzes are guided and vary throughout the book. In each *Grammar Cloze Quiz*, certain types of words are missing: articles, prepositions, verbs, or pronouns. Students can work on the quizzes individually, and then compare their answers with a partner, or they may do them alone and the teacher can check their answers.

Unit Discussion

This section contains one or two questions that help the students connect the related topics in the two chapters for that unit. The questions may be discussed in class or assigned as written homework.

Index of Key Words and Phrases

This section lists words and phrases from all the readings in the chapters for easy reference. The *Index of Key Words and Phrases* may be useful to students to help them locate words they need or wish to review.

ACKNOWLEDGMENTS

We are thankful to everyone at Heinle, especially Sherrise Roehr, Tom Jefferies, Tünde A. Dewey, and Lauren Rodan. As always, we are very appreciative of the ongoing encouragement from our family and friends.

L.C.S. and N.N.M.

Today's Travelers

CHAPTER 1

A Family Sees America Together

Prereading Preparation

1   Look at the photograph of the family. What are they planning to do?
    a. Take a weekend trip
    b. Take a short vacation
    c. Take a long vacation

2   Look at the title of the chapter. Where does the family plan to travel?
    a. Canada
    b. the United States
    c. Mexico

3   How long will their trip be? (Write a specific amount of time.)

    ~~Your~~ 1 Year the Graham family started
    their trip on July 4 they returned

4   How many miles will they travel? (Write a specific number of miles.)

    50 miles

A Family Sees America Together

1   The Graham family of Wichita, Kansas, did something very unusual last
2 year. Mr. and Mrs. Graham did not go to work, and their children did not go to
3 school. Instead, Craig and Marlene Graham and their children, Courtney, 12, and
4 Collier, 4, traveled together in a van and drove across America for a whole year.

5   First, Craig and Marlene sold their businesses. Craig had a real estate business,
6 and Marlene owned a small newspaper. Then they sold their large house. Finally,
7 Courtney said goodbye to her classmates, and their dream trip was ready to
8 begin. The Graham family started their trip on July 4, Independence Day. They
9 visited big cities and small towns in all 50 states. They also visited the birthplaces
10 of all the United States' presidents. They wanted to visit many interesting places,
11 parks, and zoos in the United States, but they also wanted to meet the American
12 people. The Grahams had many wonderful experiences. Many people were very
13 friendly and helpful to them. Some people invited the Graham family to stay in
14 their homes with them. Everyone signed their "guest book."

15   Every day, Marlene wrote reports about her family's trip. She described the
16 family's daily experiences, where they went and what they did. Courtney kept a
17 journal of her life on the road. Marlene and Courtney put their writing on their
18 website. Schoolchildren from all over the United States followed the Graham
19 family's trip by using computers at home and in school. Some children wrote
20 letters to the Graham family. Newspapers in the U.S. published stories about the
21 Grahams, and people interviewed the family on television shows.

22   At the end of the year, Craig said that they all had a wonderful trip. Courtney
23 said that she missed her friends at school, but also enjoyed the trip very much.
24 The Grahams traveled a total of 54,944 miles. They returned home on the same
25 date that they left: July 4. They plan to write a book about their travels to describe
26 everything they learned about their country and the American people.

Fact-Finding Exercise

Read the passage once. Then read the following statements. Check whether they are True or False. If a statement is false, rewrite the statement so that it is true. Then go back to the passage and find the line that supports your answer.

1 ____✓____ True _____ False The Graham family traveled across the United States together in a van.

_____

2 _____ True ____✓____ False The Graham family did not meet many friendly, helpful people.

_____

3 _____ True ____✓____ False Craig and Collier wrote reports about their trip every day.

_____

4 ____✓____ True _____ False The Graham family had a wonderful trip.

_____

5 ____✓____ True _____ False Schoolchildren used computers to follow the Grahams' trip.

_____

Skimming and Scanning Exercise

Skim through the passage. Then read the following statements. Choose the one that is the correct main idea of the reading.

    a. The Graham family liked to drive very far in a large van.

    b. The Graham family left their home and their jobs to travel across the United States for one year.

    c. The Graham family wanted to leave Kansas to find a new place to live.

Scan the passage. Work with a partner to complete the chart below about the Graham family's trip.

	Craig	Marlene	Courtney	Collier
Is this person an adult or a child?				
What did he or she do before the trip?				
What did he or she do during the trip?				
What did he or she say after the trip?				

Reading Analysis

Read each question carefully. Circle the letter or the number of the correct answer.

1 The Graham family of **Wichita, Kansas** did something very **unusual** last year.

   a. **Wichita** is a

      1. city   *city*
      2. state ✗

   b. **Kansas** is a

      1. city
      2. state

   c. **Unusual** means

      1. special, different
      2. ordinary, common ✗

2 Mr. and Mrs. Graham did not go to work, and their children did not go to school. **Instead,** Craig and Marlene Graham and their two children drove across the United States **for a whole year.**

   a. **Instead** means

      1. in place of
      2. in addition to

   b. Complete the following sentence correctly. Maria did not want to learn to play the violin. **Instead,**

      1. she learned to play the piano
      2. she tried to play the violin ✗

   c. **A whole year** is

      1. less than one year
      2. exactly one year
      3. more than one year

3 The Graham family visited big cities and small towns **in all 50 states.** How many states are there in the United States?

   a. Less than 50
   b. Exactly 50
   c. More than 50

4 They also visited the **birthplaces** of all the United States' presidents. Your **birthplace** is

   a. the place where you live
   b. the place where your children were born
   c. the place where you were born

5 Courtney **kept a journal** of her life **on the road.**

   a. Kept a journal means

     1. wrote in a journal
     2. saved a journal
     3. read a journal

   b. On the road means

     1. lying in the street
     2. traveling
     3. sitting inside a car

D Dictionary Skills

Read the dictionary entry for each word and think about the context of the sentence. Write the number of the appropriate definition on the line next to the word. Then choose the sentence with the correct answer.

> **1** **dream** *n.* **1** a fantasy experienced while asleep: *The child has bad dreams.*
> **2** s.t. hoped for, aspiration: *She has a dream about being an engineer.*
> **3** a beautiful person or thing: *They're building their dream house.*

The Graham family had a **dream** to travel across America together.

a. dream: _____
b. 1. The Graham family had fantasies in their sleep about traveling across the United States.
   2. The Graham family were all beautiful people.
   3. The Graham family hoped to travel across the United States.

2 | experience *n.* **1** [U] an event, a happening: *Our visit to Alaska was a pleasant experience.* **2** [U] understanding gained through doing s.t.: *She has years of experience in teaching.*

The Grahams had many wonderful **experiences** during their year on the road.

a. **experience:** _____

b. 1. The one-year trip across the United States was a wonderful event for the Grahams.

2. The one-year trip across the United States was a wonderful understanding for the Grahams.

3 | own *v.* **1** [T] to have as property: *She owns a bookstore.* **2** [I; T] to admit, acknowledge: *The judge owned that the juror was biased.* **3** *phrasal v. insep.* [I] **to own up to s.t.:** to confess, admit to s.t.: *The little boy finally owned up to the fact that he ate all the cookies.*

Marlene **owned** a small newspaper. She sold her business before the trip began.

a. **own:** _____

b. 1. Marlene possessed a small newspaper business. She sold her property before the trip began.

2. Marlene acknowledged a small newspaper business before the trip.

E Word Forms

In English, the noun form and the verb form of some words are the same, for example, *walk (v.), walk (n.)*. Read each sentence. Write the correct form of the word on the left. Then circle *(v.)* if you are using a verb or *(n.)* if you are using a noun. **Write all the verbs in the simple past tense. The nouns may be singular or plural.**

interview　　　　**1** John _____ the governor of Kansas last night. John
　　　　　　　　　　　　　　　　(v., n.)

　　　　　　　　did several _____ with the governor last year, too.
　　　　　　　　　　　　　(v., n.)

[C]—Countable (noun); [U]—Uncountable (noun); s.o.—someone, s.t.—something; *(syn.)*—synonym; *n.*—noun; *v.*—verb; I—Intransitive; T—Transitive

plan

2 Martha and Jim made some exciting _____ for
(v., n.)

their vacation last summer. They _____ to visit
(v., n.)

the county's capital and a national park, and they had a

wonderful time.

report

3 The weather _____ for yesterday included rain and
(v., n.)

strong winds. The weatherman _____ that many
(v., n.)

trees fell down and some houses were damaged.

work

4 Michael had a lot of _____ to do yesterday. He
(v., n.)

_____ from 8 A.M. until 10 P.M.
(v., n.)

visit

5 I have made a few _____ to the City Museum of Art.
(v., n.)

I _____ the museum four times last winter.
(v., n.)

Word Partnership	Use *visit* with:
n.	visit **family/relatives**, visit **friends**, visit *your* **mother** **weekend** visit visit **a museum**, visit **a restaurant**
v.	**come to** visit, **go to** visit, **invite** *someone* **to** visit, **plan to** visit
adj.	**brief** visit, **last** visit, **next** visit, **recent** visit, **short** visit, **surprise** visit, **foreign** visit, **official** visit

Vocabulary in Context

helpful *(adj.)*	interview *(v.)*	plans *(v.)*	unusual *(adj.)*
helpful *(adj.)*	interview *(v.)*	plans *(v.)*	unusual *(adj.)*
instead *(adv.)*	owns *(v.)*	travel *(v.)*	whole *(adj.)*

Read the following sentences. Complete each blank space with the correct word from the list above. Use each word only once.

1 Most companies _____ people before giving them a job.

2 My family and I always _____ together. Last year, we took a trip to New York.

3 My brother and I want to go to the beach, but it's too cold today. We are going to the movies _____.

4 After Maria learns English, she _____ to get a good job in this city.

5 Yuki lived in New York for a _____ year. She enjoyed her twelve months in the United States.

6 Our teacher is very _____. She answers all our questions and teaches us new words.

7 Santiago never takes the bus because he _____ a car.

8 The weather is very _____ today. It was sunny in the morning. Then it rained in the afternoon. Now it is snowing!

Think About It

Read the following questions and think about the answers. Write your answer below each question. Then compare your answers with those of your classmates.

1 Newspapers in the U.S. published stories about the Grahams. People interviewed the family on television shows. Why did people want to know about the Grahams' trip?

_____

_____

_____

_____

_____

_____

_____

2 Courtney Graham did not go to school for a whole year. Do you think her teachers were angry? Why or why not?

_____

_____

_____

_____

_____

_____

_____

Another Look

Look at the map. Read Courtney's journal entry describing her family's visit to Texas. Then answer the questions on the next page.

Courtney's Texas—Big History, Big Cities, Big Hearts

1   Texas is a big state. The first town we visited was El Paso. Two other neat towns
2 were San Antonio and Austin. Austin is the capital city. It's very modern, very
3 technology-oriented, and is really growing. We visited the capitol building there.
4 Photographers from the ABC television station in Austin met us at the capitol and
5 took some shots of us looking around.
6   After Austin, we headed on to San Antonio. We got to stay at the Marriott on the
7 Riverwalk. The manager heard about our trip and let us stay for a night. That was so
8 nice! They even gave us cheese and fruit. Wow! We felt so welcome.
9   In San Antonio, we also got to see the Alamo. Hard to believe this is where Davy
10 Crockett died. All those people in the Battle of the Alamo were so brave, especially
11 since many of them weren't Texans, just other guys trying to help the Texans gain
12 their freedom from Mexico. Davy Crockett and his fighters were from Tennessee.
13 Inside the Alamo, you can see some of the actual guns that were used. A television
14 crew from the ABC station in San Antonio did a story with us, too. It was kind of neat
15 to be filmed at the Alamo.
16   Of course, you've heard of other big cities in Texas like Houston. We had planned on
17 spending some time there with a family we had met over the Internet, but we didn't
18 make it to Houston because we were trying to get back on schedule.
19   There are a lot of neat places in Texas. This is a really cool state. But then if you're
20 from Texas, you already know that.

Questions for Another Look

1 Courtney wrote that Texas has a big history, big cities, and big hearts.

  a. Texas has a big history means that

   1. the history of Texas is very interesting
   2. the history of Texas is very large

  b. Texas has big hearts means that

   1. Texans are very friendly people
   2. Texans have hearts that are very large

2 The Graham family had two interesting experiences in Austin, Texas. What were they?

_____

_____

3 What did you learn about Texas after reading Courtney's journal? Check the information that you read about.

_____ **a.** Texas is a very big state.

_____ **b.** Texas has many mountains.

_____ **c.** Texas used to be part of Mexico.

_____ **d.** Texas has very cold weather.

_____ **e.** Davy Crockett was not from Texas.

_____ **f.** The Alamo was a famous battle in Texan history.

_____ **g.** Texans like to travel.

4 Does Courtney like Texas?

  a. Yes
  b. No

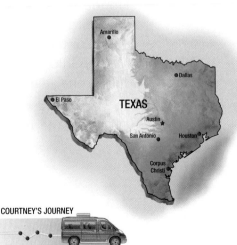

COURTNEY'S JOURNEY

Topics for Discussion and Writing

1 Pretend that you will take a trip in the United States. Write a paragraph. Describe where you will go. What will you visit there?

2 Do you think it is a good idea to travel in a van with your family? Why is it a good idea? Why is it a bad idea?

3 **Write in your journal.** Describe a trip that you took alone or with your family. Did you enjoy it? Why or why not?

Follow-Up Activities

1 The Grahams' trip took one year, and they traveled 54,944 miles. Check the guesses you made on page 2. Which student in the class guessed the length and distance of the trip the most accurately?

2 The Graham family began their trip on July 4. They traveled to the 50 states in the following order: Kansas, Nebraska, Iowa, Wisconsin, Minnesota, North Dakota, South Dakota, Wyoming, Montana, Alaska, Washington, Oregon, Idaho, Utah, Colorado, Nevada, California, Hawaii, Arizona, New Mexico, Texas, Oklahoma, Arkansas, Louisiana, Mississippi, Alabama, Florida, Georgia, South Carolina, North Carolina, Tennessee, Kentucky, West Virginia, Virginia, Maryland, Delaware, Pennsylvania, New Jersey, New York, Connecticut, Rhode Island, Massachusetts, Vermont, New Hampshire, Maine, Ohio, Indiana, Michigan, Illinois, Missouri. They ended their trip on July 4, one year later in Kansas.

   a. Look at the map of the United States, and then trace the family's route on the map on the next page.

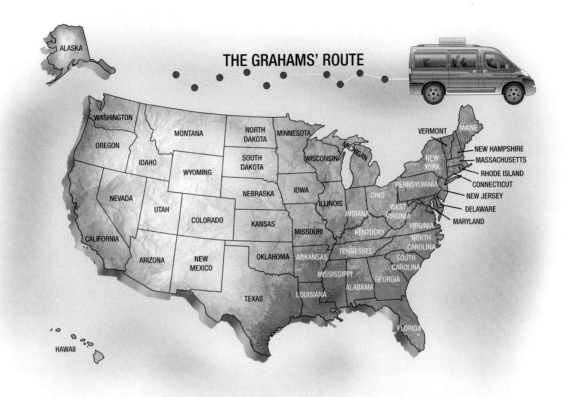

THE GRAHAMS' ROUTE

b. Read the list below. Check the reasons you think the Graham family followed this route.

_____ 1. Because of the weather

_____ 2. Because they liked some states better than other states

_____ 3. Because many of the states were next to each other

_____ 4. Because they wanted to visit their family

_____ 5. Because this route was the most direct

_____ 6. Because they got lost several times

K Word Search

Read the words listed below. Find them in the puzzle and circle them. They may be written in any direction.

dreams	Internet	planning	unusual
experiences	interview	report	visit
instead	journal	travels	works

```
E  X  P  E  R  I  E  N  C  E  S  I  J  E  W
F  K  L  M  H  Q  N  P  D  S  N  Q  N  F  O
L  O  A  O  J  U  V  T  A  T  M  S  P  A  R
U  X  N  O  A  O  G  O  E  G  N  A  Z  Q  K
J  O  N  S  C  A  U  R  T  R  A  V  E  L  S
B  O  I  L  R  N  N  R  S  I  V  E  D  R  N
V  E  N  N  U  E  Y  C  N  M  S  I  W  I  D
E  Q  G  S  T  P  P  X  I  A  U  I  E  D  L
G  A  U  N  E  X  T  O  D  Z  L  F  V  W  C
V  A  P  A  S  H  N  W  R  X  K  E  E  T  P
L  V  R  Y  J  R  O  Q  O  T  B  F  X  T  X
```

Crossword Puzzle

Read the clues on the next page. Write the answers in the correct spaces in the puzzle.

Crossword Puzzle Clues

ACROSS CLUES

4. Our class ends _____ 2 o'clock.

6. Newspapers _____, or print information

7. Not typical; not usual

8. We _____; she has

10. You write your personal experiences in a _____.

12. The city or town you were born in is your _____.

17. Real estate is a kind of _____.

19. John isn't here _____. He'll be here in a few minutes.

21. People ask other people questions in an _____ for television or the newspaper.

25. A _____ is something you hope for all your life.

27. Pleasant; agreeable

28. The past tense of **put**

DOWN CLUES

1. The opposite of **down**

2. The other students in your class are your _____.

3. He _____ a teacher in our school.

5. To take a trip

7. **I, me; we,** _____

9. The opposite of **yes**

11. John wrote his name from left to right _____ the top of his paper.

13. Courtney Graham didn't study in school. _____, she studied during her trip.

14. I will meet you _____ 3:30.

15. An _____ is something that happens to you.

16. I wear glasses, _____ Debbie doesn't.

18. The _____ is a system of computers around the world.

20. The opposite of **no**

22. I am going _____ the store.

23. A large automobile

24. You and I

26. **I,** _____; **he, him**

Grammar Cloze Quiz

Read the story. Then use the pronouns to fill in the blanks. You may use each pronoun more than once.

they

her	she	their	them

   Every day Marlene wrote reports about **their** family's trip. **She** (1) (2) described the family's daily experiences, where **she** went and what they (3) did. Courtney kept a journal of **her** life on the road. Marlene and Courtney (4) put **their** writing on the Internet. At the end of the year, Craig said that (5) **they** all had a wonderful trip. Courtney missed **her** friends at school, (6) (7) but **she** also enjoyed the trip very much. The Grahams traveled a total (8) of 54,944 miles. **They** returned home on the same date that they left. The (9) family plans to write a book about **their** travels. (10)

CHAPTER 2

Volunteer Vacations

Prereading Preparation

1 What are volunteers?

People voluhteer they are help other people without desire.

2 What kinds of work do volunteers do? Work in a small group. Use the diagram below to help you organize your answers. When you are finished, share your answers with the class.

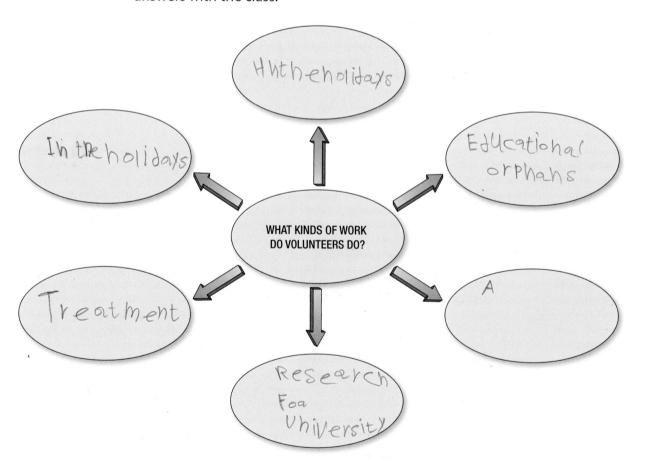

Huth.enholidays

In the holidays

Educational orphans

WHAT KINDS OF WORK DO VOLUNTEERS DO?

Treatment

A

Research Foa Uhiversity

3 Look at the photograph below. What are these people doing?

_____

4 Who do you think they are building the house for?

_____

5 What are some reasons that people volunteer to help others?

_____

Volunteer Vacations

1   Everyone enjoys taking a vacation. A vacation is fun and relaxing. Some
2 people like to go to the beach and swim. Other people go to the mountains or
3 visit another country. Many other people use their vacation time for another
4 reason. What do they do? They take a volunteer vacation to help other people.
5 Volunteers are people who do something, but they receive no money for it. They
6 do this because they want to be helpful to people in need. Many organizations
7 give volunteers a chance to help others.
8   Habitat for Humanity is one of these organizations. Habitat for Humanity is
9 an organization of volunteers who build homes for the poor. The most famous
10 volunteer is former U.S. President Jimmy Carter, who won the Nobel Prize for
11 Peace. Habitat for Humanity volunteers don't need a special skill. They just
12 need to be in good health. Volunteers build homes in the United States, but they

also construct homes all over the world, in places such as Honduras, Fiji, and Ethiopia. Volunteers pay for their own trips. For example, a two-week trip to Honduras, Fiji, or Ethiopia is about $1,200.

A second volunteer organization is called Earthwatch. Earthwatch gets many volunteers to help scientists do research in many places around the world. For example, volunteers may study endangered animals, such as manatees in Florida. Most of the trips are two weeks. Volunteers pay about $1,800 to participate, without airfare. They usually stay in dormitories and cook their meals together. This year, Earthwatch had 4,000 volunteers from 47 different countries.

Cross-Cultural Solutions is another volunteer organization. It helps communities in China, Ghana, India, Peru, and Russia. Cross-Cultural Solutions helps to bring health care and education to many people. Twelve to eighteen volunteers work together for about three weeks at one location. The work depends on the volunteers' skills. For instance, a volunteer may have special medical knowledge. This person will work in a local hospital. Volunteers have evenings and two weekends to spend on their own. Prices begin at $1,900 for a two-week trip, not including airfare.

People who take volunteer vacations believe they are helping people around the world to live healthier lives. They believe they can help people get an education. The people they help may have a better place to live. For the volunteers, this is the best vacation of all.

Fact-Finding Exercise

Read the passage once. Then read the following statements. Check whether they are True or False. If a statement is false, change the statement so that it is true. Then go back to the passage and find the line that supports your answer.

1 _____ True _____ False Volunteer vacations are fun and relaxing.

_____

2 _____ True _____ False Habitat for Humanity volunteers build houses all around the world.

_____

3 _____ True _____ False Former U.S. President Jimmy Carter helps build houses for poor people.

_____

4 _____ True _____ False Earthwatch helps doctors take care of people.

_____

5 _____ True _____ False Cross-Cultural Solutions helps people with education.

_____

6 _____ True _____ False All volunteer organizations pay the volunteers.

_____

7 _____ True _____ False Volunteers pay for their own airfare.

_____

8 _____ True _____ False Volunteer vacations are usually for only a week.

_____

Skimming and Scanning Exercise

PART 1

Skim through the passage. Then read the following statements. Choose the one that is the correct main idea of the reading.

a. Vacation volunteers receive money for helping people all around the world build their own homes.

b. Vacation volunteers work with organizations to help people around the world live better lives.

c. Vacation volunteers travel around the world to have fun and to relax in different countries.

PART 2

Work in small groups and complete the chart about Volunteer Vacations.

	What do they do?	Where do they work?	How long is a volunteer vacation?	How much does it cost?
Habitat for Humanity				
Earthwatch				
Cross-Cultural Solutions				

Reading Analysis

Read each question carefully. Circle the letter or the number of the correct answer.

1. **Volunteers** are people who do something, but they receive no money for it. They do this because they want to be helpful to other **people in need.**

    a. **Volunteers** are people who
        1. work without pay
        2. need other people
        3. need some help

    b. **People in need**
        1. want someone to do something for them
        2. cannot always help themselves
        3. volunteer to help others

2. Volunteers need to be in good health. They build homes in the United States, but they also **construct** homes all over the world.

    Construct means

    a. volunteer
    b. condition
    c. build

3. Earthwatch gets many volunteers to help scientists do **research** in places around the world.

    Research means

    a. to study something carefully
    b. to do volunteer work
    c. to travel to different places

4. Earthwatch volunteers usually stay in **dormitories** and cook their meals together.

    Dormitories are

    a. individual homes
    b. homes for groups of people
    c. hotels

5 Twelve to eighteen volunteers work together for about three weeks at one **location.**

A **location** is a

a. job
b. place
c. person

6 Prices for Cross-Cultural Solutions **begin at** $1,900 for a two-week trip, not including airfare.

a. **Begin at** $1,900 means

1. $1,900 is the highest price
2. $1,900 is the usual price
3. $1,900 is the lowest price

b. A two-week trip

1. will cost at least $1,900. You also need to buy your own airplane ticket.
2. will usually cost $1,900. Your airplane ticket is part of the cost.
3. will always cost $1,900. You also need to buy your own airplane ticket.

D Dictionary Skills

Read the dictionary entry for each word and think about the context of the sentence. Write the number of the appropriate definition on the line next to the word. Then choose the sentence with the correct answer.

---

1 **former** *adj.* **1** previous, past: *He is a former employee of this company.* **2** referring to the first thing or person named in a pair
—*n.* the first thing or person named in a pair: *We eat lots of fish and chicken, but we prefer the former* (meaning "the fish").

The most famous volunteer is **former** U.S. President Jimmy Carter.

a. **former:** _____
b. 1. The most famous volunteer is the past U.S. President Jimmy Carter.
   2. The most famous volunteer is the first in a pair of U.S. Presidents, Jimmy Carter.

2 | **skill** *n.* [C; U] **1** an ability to do s.t. well because of practice, talent, or special training: *She has excellent musical skills.* **2** a trade: *Plumbing is his skill.*

A volunteer for Cross-Cultural Solutions may have a **skill,** for example, special medical knowledge. This person will work in a local hospital.

a. **skill:** _____
b. 1. A volunteer may have the ability to do something well because of special training.
    2. A volunteer may have a trade.

Word Forms

In English, there are several ways that verbs change to nouns. Some verbs become nouns by adding the suffix *-tion,* for example, *collect (v.), collection (n.).* Some words change spelling, for example, *explain (v.), explanation (n.).* Complete each sentence with the correct form of the words on the left. **Write all the verbs in the simple present tense. They may be affirmative or negative. The nouns may be singular or plural.**

educate *(v.)*   **1** People around the world want all children to have a good

education *(n.)*   _____. We usually _____ children

in schools and at home.

locate *(v.)*   **2** Volunteer organizations _____ communities

location *(n.)*   in need. The _____ for volunteer work are

usually in developing countries.

construct *(v.)*   **3** The _____ of a new home can be very

construction *(n.)*   fast when many volunteers work together. They

_____ homes in many cities around the world.

[C]—Countable (noun); [U]—Uncountable (noun); s.o.—someone, s.t.—something; *(syn.)*—synonym; *n.*—noun; *v.*—verb; I—Intransitive; T—Transitive

organize (v.)

organization (n.)

4 When a volunteer _____ works well, it helps many people. Habitat for Humanity _____ groups of workers to build houses for people who cannot afford them.

solve (v.)

solution (n.)

5 Chris _____ his problems slowly. He thinks quickly. He thinks of several _____ right away, then chooses the best one.

Word Partnership	Use *solve* with:
n.	**ability to** solve *something*, solve **a crisis,** solve **a mystery,** solve **a problem,** solve **a puzzle, way to** solve *something*
v.	**attempt/try to** solve *something*, **help** solve *something*

Word Partnership	Use *solution* with:
adj.	**best** solution, **peaceful** solution, **perfect** solution, **possible** solution, **practical** solution, **temporary** solution, **easy** solution, **obvious** solution, **simple** solution
prep.	solution **to a conflict,** solution **to a crisis,** solution **to a problem**
v.	**propose a** solution, **reach a** solution, **seek a** solution, **find a** solution

Vocabulary in Context

احتفال *(Arabic handwriting)* ... *(Arabic handwriting)*

(Arabic handwriting) ... *(Arabic handwriting)* ... *(Arabic handwriting)* ... *(Arabic handwriting)*

construct *(v.)* 4	former *(adj.)* 2	research *(v.)* 8	vacation *(n.)* 5
dormitory *(n.)* 1	healthy *(adj.)* 6	skill *(n.)* 7	volunteer *(v.)* 3

(Arabic handwriting) ... *(Arabic handwriting)* ... *(Arabic handwriting)* ... *(Arabic handwriting)*

Read the following sentences. Complete each blank space with the correct word from the list above. Use each word only once.

1. Kim is a university student. He lives in a _dormitory_ at school.

2. John is the _former_ head of the company. He stopped working here last year.

3. I work at a hospital after school. I don't work for money because I _volunteer_ to help there.

4. There are a lot of children in my city. The government must _construct_ new schools for all the children.

5. My mother is a very hard worker. She needs to take a _vacation_ so that she can relax.

6. My parents are very _healthy_ people. They eat well, exercise every day, and are never sick.

7. Justin is an excellent cook. He learned this _skill_ from his grandmother.

8. Scientists _research_ food that is good for us. They learned that fruit and vegetables are good for our health, so we eat them often.

Think About It

Read the questions and think about the answers. Write your answer for each question. Then compare your answers with those of your classmates.

1 Former U.S. President Jimmy Carter is a volunteer for Habitat for Humanity. Why do you think he volunteers to help build houses for poor people?

_____

_____

_____

_____

_____

_____

_____

2 Why do many people work so hard to help people they do not know, in countries they do not live in? What do you think?

_____

_____

_____

_____

_____

_____

_____

Another Look

Read the following story about people who do volunteer work. Then answer the questions that follow.

Track 4

Who Volunteers?

1   People volunteer in order to help other people in need. They also volunteer
2   in order to "give back" to the community. This means that they want to help the
3   people in their community who need help. However, volunteering is not only
4   good for the community and those in need, but it is good for the volunteers,
5   too. Volunteer Canada, an organization in Canada, started National Volunteer
6   Week in 1943. Today, it is still very popular. In fact, six million people around the
7   country volunteer.

8   Who volunteers? All kinds of people volunteer. For example, senior citizens
9   (people over 65 years old) volunteer for many reasons. They want to meet new
10 friends and stay active. Senior citizens often have a lot of free time. They can use
11 this time to help other people. Sometimes, when people graduate from college,
12 they do volunteer work. Then they can get some skills and experience before
13 they find a job. Other people volunteer because it gives them a chance to do
14 something different. New immigrants to Canada also volunteer. They get work
15 experience and can improve their English and French language skills.

16   All of these volunteers in Canada do different work, but they have something
17 in common: they are helping other people. And by helping other people, they
18 are helping themselves, too.

Questions for Another Look

1 Who are **senior citizens?**
   a. Volunteers
   b. People over 65 years old
   c. College graduates

2 Who are **immigrants?**
   a. People who come from another country
   b. People who live in Canada
   c. People who volunteer

3 Who started National Volunteer Week in Canada?

_____

4 Look at the chart below. Why do these people volunteer? Write the reasons.

Volunteers	Why do they volunteer?
1. Senior citizens	
2. College graduates	
3. New immigrants	

Topics for Discussion and Writing الى هنا

1 This chapter discusses three volunteer organizations. Which one do you think does the most important work? Why? Write your reasons and give examples.

2 Former U.S. President Jimmy Carter is very famous. Do you think it is a good idea for famous people to volunteer to help others? Why? Explain your reasons.

3 What was your favorite vacation? Why? Who did you go with? Write about what you did on your favorite vacation.

4 **Write in your journal.** Will you ever volunteer to work with an organization, such as Habitat for Humanity, Earthwatch, or Cross-Cultural Solutions? If so, which one? Why? If not, why not?

Follow-Up Activities

1 Work in a group. What can volunteers do for people in need? Make a list.

- *Build homes*

-

-

-

2 Work in pairs. Imagine you are going to interview the director of National Volunteer Week. Make a list of questions you want to ask this person. Compare your list of questions with those of your classmates.

_____

_____

_____

Word Search

Read the words listed below. Find them in the puzzle and circle them. They may be written in any direction.

airfare السفرجو	famous مشهور	location المكان	vacation عطله
construct بناء	healthy صحي	organizations المنظمات	volunteer متطوع
dormitories المعاجم	helpful زيارة المساعد	research بحث	world العالم

```
S  H  E  L  P  F  U  L  R  V  G  R  J  C  T
R  E  M  Q  T  H  X  S  A  U  Y  S  I  M  C
E  N  I  R  E  T  H  C  R  H  U  C  S  K  U
S  M  W  R  E  H  A  E  T  G  K  E  Q  Q  R
E  L  V  W  O  T  E  L  U  J  B  B  U  N  T
A  S  N  O  I  T  A  Z  I  N  A  G  R  O  S
R  V  C  O  N  E  I  L  O  C  A  T  I  O  N
C  R  N  U  H  B  D  M  T  R  R  P  P  F  O
H  X  L  M  N  B  R  L  R  N  U  I  R  G  C
H  O  S  U  O  M  A  F  R  O  W  K  H  Y  Z
V  A  U  R  H  V  R  H  T  O  D  T  X  O  H
E  R  A  F  R  I  A  I  X  V  W  F  P  H  Q
```

L Crossword Puzzle

Read the clues on the next page. Write the answers in the correct spaces in the puzzle.

Crossword Puzzle Clues

ACROSS CLUES

1. Build
5. Time off from work
8. Study something carefully
9. Previous; past
10. Answer to a problem
11. Earthwatch, Habitat for Humanity, Cross-Cultural Solutions are all _____.
13. We go to school to get an _____.
14. People who work without being paid

DOWN CLUES

2. Abilities
3. Peru, Russia, Honduras, and China are all _____.
4. An endangered animal in Florida
6. Place
7. Home for groups of people
12. The price of an airplane ticket

Grammar Cloze Quiz

Read the passage. Complete each blank space with an article from the box. You may use each article more than once.

a	an	the

Everyone enjoys taking _____ vacation. _____ vacation is fun and
(1)   (2)
relaxing. Some people like to go to _____ beach and swim. Other people go
(3)
to the mountains or visit _____ unusual country. Many other people take
(4)
_____ volunteer vacation to help other people. Volunteers are people who
(5)

do something because they want to be helpful to other people in need. Many organizations give volunteers _____ chance to help others.
(6)

Habitat for Humanity is _____ organization of volunteers who build homes for _____ poor. _____ most famous volunteer is former U.S. President Jimmy Carter, who won _____ Nobel Prize for Peace. Habitat for Humanity volunteers don't need _____ special skill. They just need to be in good health. Volunteers build homes in _____ United States, but they also construct homes all over _____ world.
(7) (8) (9) (10) (11) (12) (13)

_____ second organization is called Earthwatch. Earthwatch volunteers may study _____ endangered animal, such as manatees in Florida.
(14) (15)

UNIT 1 DISCUSSION

1. A cross-country trip is a common family vacation for Americans. How is this way of traveling all-American? How does a trip like this characterize American culture?

   _____

   _____

   _____

   _____

2. Many people around the world volunteer during their vacation to help other people. What other ways can people volunteer to help others?

   _____

   _____

   _____

   _____

Family Life

CHAPTER 3

How Alike Are Identical Twins?

Prereading Preparation

1 Look at the photograph below. Describe the two people.

2 Read the title of this passage. What will the reading tell you about?

3 Choose the sentences which describe identical twins.

_____ **a.** They are always both boys or both girls.

_____ **b.** Identical twins can be a boy and a girl.

_____ **c.** Identical twins always have the same color hair.

_____ **d.** One identical twin can have dark hair and the other can have light hair.

_____ **e.** Identical twins always have the same color eyes.

_____ **f.** One identical twin may have blue eyes and the other may have brown eyes.

_____ **g.** As adults, identical twins will be the same height.

_____ **h.** As adults, one identical twin may be taller than the other.

How Alike Are Identical Twins?

Most twins who grew up together are very close. John and Buell Fuller are 79-year-old identical twins. They have always lived together, and still do. They wear identical clothes and work together, too. They think it is funny that people can't tell them apart. In fact, they like to confuse people. Sometimes John tells people he is Buell, and sometimes Buell tells people he is John.

Identical twins like the Fullers are very unusual in the United States. Out of every 1,000 births, there are only four pairs of identical twins. Naturally, most people are very curious about them. Scientists want to know about twins, too. Do twins feel the same pain? Do they think the same thoughts? Do they share these thoughts?

Scientists understand how twins are born. Now, though, they are trying to explain how being half of a biological pair influences a twin's identity. They want to know why many identical twins make similar choices even when they don't live near each other. For example, Jim Springer and Jim Lewis are identical twins. They were separated when they were only four months old.

The two Jims grew up in different families and did not meet for 39 years. When they finally met, they discovered some surprising similarities between them. Both men were married twice. Their first wives were named Linda, and their second wives were both named Betty! Both twins named their first sons James Allan, drove blue Chevrolets, and had dogs named Toy. Are all these facts coincidences, or are they biological?

Scientists want to know what influences our personality. They study pairs of identical twins who grew up in different surroundings, like Jim Springer and Jim Lewis. These twins help scientists understand the connection between environment and biology. Researchers at the University of Minnesota studied 350 sets of identical twins who did not grow up together. They discovered many similarities in their personalities. Scientists believe that personality characteristics such as friendliness, shyness, and fears are not a result of environment. These characteristics are probably inherited.

Some pairs of identical twins say that they have ESP[1] experiences. For instance, some twins say that they can feel when their twin is in pain or in trouble. Twins also seem to be closer and more open to each other's thoughts and feelings than other brothers and sisters. For example, Donald and Louis Keith are close in this way. The Keiths are identical twins. Donald says that by concentrating very hard, he can make Louis telephone him.

[1]ESP: Extrasensory Perception. ESP is the ability to feel something that people cannot feel with the five senses.

36	Scientists continue to study identical twins because they are uncertain about
37	them and have many questions. For example, they are still unsure about the
38	connection between environment and personality. They want to know: can twins
39	really communicate without speaking? Can one twin really feel another twin's
40	pain? Perhaps with more research, scientists will find the answers.

Fact-Finding Exercise

Read the passage once. Then read the following statements. Check whether they are True or False. If a statement is false, rewrite the statement so that it is true. Then go back to the passage and find the line that supports your answer.

1 _____ True _____ False   Scientists want to know about identical twins.

_____

2 _____ True _____ False   Jim Springer and Jim Lewis always lived together.

_____

3 _____ True _____ False Scientists understand twins better when they study twins who grew up together.

_____

4 _____ True _____ False John and Buell Fuller were separated at birth and did not grow up together.

_____

5 _____ True _____ False Some identical twins have ESP experiences about each other.

_____

6 _____ True _____ False Scientists believe that people are born with friendly, shy, or fearful personalities.

_____

B

Skimming and Scanning Exercise

PART 1

Skim through the passage. Then read the following statements. Choose the one that is the correct main idea of the reading.

a. John and Buell Fuller, typical identical twins, grew up together.
b. Identical twins are very unusual in the United States.
c. Doctors believe that identical twins are very similar in both their looks and their personalities.

Scan the passage. Work with a partner to fill in the chart with information from the reading.

IDENTICAL TWINS		
	Their Names	Similarities between Them
Twins Who Grew Up Together		
Twins Who Grew Up Apart		
University of Minnesota Study a. Which identical twins did the researchers study? b. How many sets of twins did researchers study? c. Why did researchers study them?	a. b. c.	
What characteristics of twins may be inherited?		

C

Reading Analysis

Read each question carefully. Either circle the letter or the number of the correct answer, or write your answer in the space provided.

1 Most twins who grew up together are very **close.** John and Buell Fuller are 79-year-old identical twins. They have always lived together, and **still do.** They wear identical clothes and work together, too. They think it is amusing that people **can't tell them apart.**

    a. In this paragaraph, **close** means that they

        1. live near each other

        2. live in the same house

        3. are very good friends

b. What do John and Buell Fuller **still do?**

   1. Confuse people

   2. Live together

   3. Wear the same clothes

c. People **can't tell them apart.** This means that

   1. they look exactly the same

   2. people can't talk to them alone

   3. they never work apart

2 Out of every 1,000 births, there are only four pairs of identical twins. This sentence means that

   a. if 1,000 women have babies, four women will have identical twins

   b. only four pairs of identical twins are born in the U.S. every year

3 Most people **are very curious** about identical twins. Scientists want to know about twins, too. Do twins feel the same pain? Do they think the same thoughts? Do they share these thoughts?

In these sentences, which word or phrase is a synonym for **are very curious?**

   a. Feel

   b. Want to know

   c. Think

4 Scientists understand how twins are born. Now, though, they are trying to explain how **being half of a biological pair** influences a twin's identity.

Being half of a biological pair means being

   a. a scientist

   b. a twin

   c. alone

5 Jim Springer and Jim Lewis are famous identical twins. They were separated when they were only four months old. The **two Jims** grew up in different families and did not meet for 39 years. **Both** men were married twice. Their first wives were named Linda and their second wives were **both** named Betty!

   a. Who are the **two Jims?**

_____

b. How many is **both?**

1. Two
2. Four
3. Six

6 Both Jim Springer and Jim Lewis named their first sons James Allan. Both Jims drove blue Chevrolets. They both had dogs named Toy. Are all these facts simply **coincidences?**

a. A **coincidence** is something that happens

1. by plan, or arrangement
2. by accident, or chance

b. Read the following sentences. Decide which situation is a coincidence.

1. Dean telephoned Jenny and invited her to have lunch with him. They decided to meet at 1 o'clock in front of The Palace Restaurant. Jenny arrived at 1 o'clock, and Dean arrived at 1:05. They said "Hi" to each other, and went into the restaurant.
2. Dean and Jenny sat at a table in the restaurant. Jenny saw her sister, Christine, at the next table! Jenny and Christine greeted each other, and they all had lunch together at the same table.

7 Scientists want to know what influences our personality. **Pairs** of identical twins who grew up in different **surroundings,** like Jim Springer and Jim Lewis, help scientists understand the connection between environment and biology. Researchers at the University of Minnesota studied 350 sets of identical twins who did not grow up together.

a. In this paragraph, which word is a synonym of **pairs?**

_____

b. In this paragraph, which word is a synonym of **surroundings?**

_____

c. What does the word in answer "b" mean?

1. The house you live in
2. The place you live in
3. The people you live with
4. All of the above

8 Scientists believe that personality characteristics such as friendliness, shyness, and fears are not a result of environment. **They** are inherited.

    a. What are some examples of personality characteristics?

    _____

    b. How do you know?

    _____

    c. What does **they** refer to?
        1. Scientists
        2. Personality characteristics
        3. Fears

9 Other pairs of identical twins say that they have **ESP** experiences.

    a. Look at page 41. What is **ESP?**

    _____

    b. How do you know?

    _____

    c. This type of information is called a
        1. preface
        2. footnote
        3. direction

10 Donald and Louis Keith are very close. **The Keiths** are identical twins. Donald says that **by concentrating very hard, he can make Louis telephone him.**

    a. Who are **the Keiths?**

    _____

    b. What does Donald mean?
        1. Donald tells Louis to call him, and Louis calls him.
        2. Donald thinks about Louis, and Louis calls him.

11 Scientists continue to study identical twins because they are **uncertain** about them and have many questions. However, most twins are sure about one fact: being a twin is wonderful because you are never alone and you always have a best friend!

In this paragraph, what word means the opposite of **uncertain?**

_____

Dictionary Skills

Read the dictionary entry for each word and think about the context of the sentence. Write the number of the appropriate definition on the line next to the word. Then choose the sentence with the correct answer.

1

> **concentrate** *v.* **-trated, -trating, -trates** **1** [I] to think hard about s.t., (*syn.*) to focus one's attention: *During exams, students concentrate hard on answering the questions.* **2** [T] to reduce the amount of s.t. and increase its strength, (*syn.*) to condense: *Orange juice that is concentrated can be stored in the freezer.*
> —*n.* [C; U] a condensed form of s.t.: *a chemical concentrate*

Donald and Louis Keith are identical twins. Donald says that by **concentrating** very hard, he can make Louis telephone him.

a. **concentrate:** _____

b. 1. Donald says that by increasing his strength, he can make Louis telephone him.

2. Donald says that by focusing his attention on Louis, he can make Louis telephone him.

3. Donald says that by reducing the amount of his strength, he can make Louis telephone him.

[C]—Countable (noun); [U]—Uncountable (noun); s.o.—someone, s.t.—something; *(syn.)*—synonym; *n.*—noun; *v.*—verb; I—Intransitive; T—Transitive

2 **close** (1) *adj.* **closer, closest** **1** with little space between, nearby: *Her chair is close to the wall.* **2** near in time: *It's close to 5:00.* **3** very friendly: *They are a close family with a few close friends.* **4** with air that is not fresh and is usu. too warm: *It is very close in this room; let's open a window.* **5** with strict control: *The doctor put her patient under close observation.* **6** **a close call:** **a** s.t. that is difficult to judge: *The two runners crossed the finish line together, so who won was a close call* (or) *too close to call.* **b** a narrow escape from danger or death: *The speeding taxi nearly hit him; that was a close call* (or) *a close shave.* *-adv.* **closely;** *-n.* **closeness.**

Twins also seem to be **closer** and more open to each other's thoughts and feelings than other brothers and sisters. For example, Donald and Louis Keith are identical twins, and they are **close** in this way.

a. **close:** _____
b. 1. Donald and Louis are intimate in this way.
   2. Donald and Louis are nearby in this way.
   3. Donald and Louis are stuffy in this way.

3 **environment** *n.* **1** [C;U] the air, land, water, and surroundings that people, plants, and animals live in: *The environment in big cities is usually polluted.* **2** [C] a set of social conditions that affect people, an atmosphere: *That child is growing up in a bad environment.* *-adj.* **environmental;** *-adv.* **environmentally.**

Scientists study pairs of identical twins who grew up in different surroundings, like Jim Springer and Jim Lewis. These twins help scientists understand the connection between biology and **environment.**

a. **environment:** _____
b. 1. Identical twins who did not grow up together help scientists understand the connection between biology and the air, land, water, and surroundings that twins live in.
   2. Identical twins who did not grow up together help scientists understand the connection between biology and the social conditions that affect people.

Word Forms

In English, some adjectives become nouns by adding the suffix -ness, for example, loud (adj.), loudness (n.). Be careful of spelling changes, for example, dry (adj.), dryness (n.), but happy (adj.), happiness (n.). Complete each sentence with the correct form of the words on the left. **The nouns are all singular.**

close (adj.)

closeness (n.)

1 Winnie and Loretta are good friends. They are

very _____ and tell each other everything.

Their _____ will continue for many years.

sure (adj.)

sureness (n.)

2 Jonathan is absolutely _____ that the movie begins

at 9:30. Because of his _____, we left for the movie

theater at 8:30.

open (adj.)

openness (n.)

3 Jimmy has a special _____ that many people like.

He makes friends easily with his warm, _____

personality.

friendly (adj.)

friendliness (n.)

4 All the people at Jodi's party are very _____ to me.

Their _____ makes me feel comfortable, and I'm

having a good time.

shy (adj.)

shyness (n.)

5 Unfortunately, Raymond's _____ stops him from

making friends. He is too _____ to talk to people he

doesn't know.

In English, the noun form and the verb form of some words are the same, for example, *cover (v.), cover (n.)*. Write the correct form of the word on the left. Then circle *(v.)* if you are using a verb or *(n.)* if you are using a noun. **Write all the verbs in the simple present tense. The verbs may be negative or positive. The nouns may be singular or plural.**

influence

1 Our parents often have a strong _____ on our lives.
(v., n.)

They usually _____ us in positive ways.
(v., n.)

fear

2 Tom has very few _____. However, when Tom
(v., n.)

goes to bed, he always _____ that he will die in
(v., n.)

his sleep.

work

3 Lisa _____ at night. She only works during the
(v., n.)

day. Her _____ is very interesting. She writes
(v., n.)

educational computer programs.

telephone

4 Please answer the _____. It is ringing. I think it is my
(v., n.)

brother. He _____ me every day at this time.
(v., n.)

experience   (5)   Sometimes a twin _____ an ESP event. When he
                                     (v., n.)

does, he usually calls his twin to see if his twin had the

same _____.
          (v., n.)

Word Partnership	Use *experience* with:
adj.	**professional** experience, **valuable** experience, **past** experience, **shared** experience, **learning** experience, **religious** experience, **traumatic** experience
n.	**work** experience, **life** experience, experience **a loss**, experience **symptoms**

F Vocabulary in Context

both *(adj.)*	**coincidence** *(n.)*	**curious** *(adj.)*	**identical** *(adj.)*
close *(adj.)*	**concentrate** *(v.)*	**environment** *(n.)*	**uncertain** *(adj.)*

Read the following sentences. Complete each blank space with the correct word from the list above. Use each word only once.

(1) Yesterday I saw our teacher on the bus. It was a _____. She was

going to the movies, and I was going to the library.

(2) I like to study in my room or at the library because _____

places are very quiet.

3 I _____ very hard when I do my homework, so I never listen to music.

4 Leigh and her sister are very _____. They share everything, and go everywhere together.

5 I am _____ about the weather today. It may rain, so I will bring my umbrella to school.

6 Our reading books are _____. They are exactly the same.

7 John loves going to the mountains. It is a very quiet, healthy _____.

8 I was very _____ about our new classmate, so I asked her some questions. She was very happy to answer me.

G Think About It

Read the following questions and think about the answers. Write your answer below each question. Then, compare your answers with those of your classmates.

1 Scientists want to study identical twins who did not grow up together. They want to understand the connection between environment and biology. Why are these identical twins so helpful to scientists?

_____

_____

_____

_____

_____

_____

2 Scientists believe that friendliness, shyness, and fears are inherited. What personality characteristics do you think are the result of environment?

_____

_____

_____

_____

_____

_____

H Another Look

Read a father's diary about the birth of his triplets and their life experiences. Then answer the questions that follow.

Track 6

Diary of a Triplet Father

1 **Birth to six months:** When the doctor told us that we were pregnant with
2 triplets, we were surprised, and wondered what the future would be. We quickly found
3 out after we brought our three babies home.
4 The first six months of parenthood is a difficult learning experience. We wrote
5 everything down, especially feeding times and how much food the babies ate. We even
6 had to chart diaper changes (960 the first month!). We marked all the toys, bottles,
7 and clothes with a different color for each child so they could sense what is theirs.
8 **Six months to four years:** It was hardest for us to get used to all the equipment.
9 We had three of everything: car seats, portable cribs, high chairs, diaper bags, and
10 changes of clothes, not to mention toys!

11   At this time of life, every minute is a new discovery. Even though you try very hard,
12 you will never be able to carefully watch all three of them at once! Every two-year-old
13 must touch and taste everything, but everything must also be shared by the triplets.
14 We soon learned that they each wanted whatever their sibling had at that moment.
15   When they began to speak, my wife noticed that they had their own names for
16 each other. When we began to make note of the particular sounds that they said to
17 each other, we realized that they had their own language. The age that we have the
18 happiest memories of is two.
19   **School age:** When it was time to send the children to school, they went to three
20 different classes. Kindergarten and first grade were easier for the kids than they
21 were for us. They each had plenty of arts and crafts homework. Since they had three
22 different assignments, homework lasted a long time. Second grade seems to be less of
23 a problem at homework time because they are able to do more work without our help.
24   The triplets don't always get along. Sometimes they fight just like other brothers
25 and sisters. However, there is still a bond between them that my wife and I hope
26 never disappears.

Questions for Another Look

Read the following list of **Life Experiences.** Put them in the correct category on the lines below.

1. Homework lasted a long time because they had different assignments.

2. The triplets had their own language.

3. The parents wrote down feeding times and how much food each baby ate.

4. It was hard for the parents to get used to all the equipment.

5. The parents wrote down diaper changes.

6. Homework time became easier in second grade because the triplets needed less help.

7. The triplets touch and taste everything.

8. The triplets had their own names for each other.

9. The parents marked all toys, clothes, and bottles with a different color.

10. Each triplet wants what the other one has.

11. The triplets each went to different kindergarten classes.

Birth to Six Months	Six Months to Four Years	School Age
_____	_____	_____
_____	_____	_____
_____	_____	_____
_____	_____	_____
_____	_____	_____

Topics for Discussion and Writing

1 Do you know any twins or triplets? Write about them. Tell who they are. Describe how they are alike and how they are different.

2 Explain why you think being a twin may be a positive or a negative experience. Explain your positive reasons and your negative reasons.

3 **Write in your journal.** Imagine that you have a twin brother or sister. What do you like best about having a twin? What do you like least about having a twin?

J

Follow-Up Activities

1 Work in pairs. Imagine you are going to interview a set of identical twins. These twins *did not* grow up together. In fact, they did not meet until they were 30 years old. Make up a list of questions to ask the twins. You want to find out how they are similar. Compare your list of questions with those of your classmates.

_____

_____

_____

2 Work in pairs. Imagine you are going to interview a set of identical twins. These twins *did* grow up together. Make up a list of questions to ask the twins. You want to find out how they are similar. Compare your list of questions with those of your classmates.

_____

_____

_____

3 If you can find a set of twins or triplets, interview them. Use the questions from #1 and #2 above. Report back to the class.

Word Search

Read the words listed below. Find them in the puzzle and circle them. They may be written in any direction.

alike	confuse	identical	personality
biological	different	influence	separate
concentrate	environment	inherited	twins

E	N	V	I	R	O	N	M	E	N	T	Y	E	I	O
L	E	K	I	L	A	U	C	B	N	T	T	R	N	A
R	A	O	T	W	I	N	S	E	I	A	H	L	H	N
L	F	C	Z	K	E	W	R	L	R	L	A	R	E	K
U	R	Q	I	U	R	E	A	T	H	C	Q	T	R	M
V	Q	Z	L	G	F	N	N	A	I	C	A	B	I	X
X	N	F	G	F	O	E	J	T	A	R	R	C	T	H
J	N	E	I	S	C	L	N	Z	A	V	O	Y	E	W
I	E	D	R	N	G	E	O	P	Q	N	B	F	D	H
T	Y	E	O	N	D	I	E	I	F	Y	J	J	N	M
W	P	C	K	I	E	S	G	U	B	A	Y	H	A	I
L	Y	T	J	Z	Y	C	S	J	G	N	T	M	C	D
E	D	F	W	R	S	E	B	R	T	O	J	N	Q	W

Crossword Puzzle

Read the clues on the next page. Write the answers in the correct spaces in the puzzle.

Crossword Puzzle Clues

1. The opposite of **after**
5. A _____ is something that happens accidentally, without planning.
9. Saturday and Sunday are _____ days of the week.
11. Cats are very _____ animals. They want to know about everything.
12. Do you sit _____ all your classmates, or do you sit alone?
13. The opposite of **off**
14. The opposite of **up**
16. I will meet you _____ 6 o'clock.
17. The color of your hair and your eyes are _____ from your parents.
19. _____ means **exactly the same.**
21. Not sure
23. _____ are people who study something very carefully.
24. The opposite of **above**
26. People cannot live _____ water.
27. The opposite of **in front of**

2. The opposite of **under**
3. I don't want to go to the movies alone. I want to go _____ you.
4. Your _____ is your character, your way of behaving.
5. Kathy and Laura are very good friends. They are very _____.
6. When I think very hard about something, I _____ on it.
7. Our surroundings are our _____.
8. Not together; apart
10. She does not like that idea. She is _____ it. She is not in favor of it.
15. The United States is _____ Canada and Mexico.
18. Our family, our education, and our home all have an _____ on us. They all affect us.
20. Almost alike; very close in appearance
22. I received a letter _____ my friend yesterday. Tomorrow I will write a letter to her.
25. The opposite of **in**
27. We come to class _____ bus.

Grammar Cloze Quiz

Read the passage. Complete each blank space with one of the pronouns from the box. You may use the pronouns more than once.

he	his	them
him	their	they

    Scientists understand how twins are born. Now, though, _____ are trying
(1)
to explain how being half of a biological pair influences _____. _____ want
(2)   (3)
to know why many identical twins make similar choices even when _____
(4)
don't live near each other. For example, Jim Springer and Jim Lewis are
identical twins. Jim Springer was separated from Jim Lewis when _____
(5)
were only four months old. Jim Springer did not meet _____ brother, Jim
(6)
Lewis, for 39 years. When Jim Springer finally met _____, _____ discovered
(7) (8)
some similarities between _____. Both men were married twice. _____ first
(9)   (10)
wives were named Linda, and _____ second wives were both named Betty!
(11)
Both twins named _____ first sons James Allan, drove blue Chevrolets,
(12)
and had dogs named Toy. Are all these facts coincidences, or are _____
(13)
biological? How can we explain _____?
(14)

4

CHAPTER

The Search for Happiness through Adoption

Prereading Preparation

1 Look at the photograph. Describe the man and the woman. Describe the children. Do you think all the children are this man and woman's biological children? Explain your answer.

2 **Adoption** means that
   a. people have children of their own
   b. people take another person's child as their own

3 What kinds of children do people adopt? For example, do people adopt young babies, older children, boys, girls, or children from different countries?

4 Read the title. Who is searching for happiness?
   a. People who adopt children
   b. Children who are adopted
   c. The people who adopt children and the children they adopt

5 Work with one or two partners. Why do people adopt children? Why do people give up a child for adoption? Make a list of reasons. When you finish, compare your list with those of your classmates.

Reasons People Adopt a Child:	Reasons People Give up a Child for Adoption:

Track 7

The Search for Happiness through Adoption

1   When couples get married, they usually plan to have children. Sometimes,
2 however, a couple cannot have a child of their own. In this case, they may decide
3 to adopt a child. In fact, adoption is very common today. There are about 130,000
4 adoptions each year in the United States alone. Some people prefer to adopt
5 infants; others adopt older children. Some couples adopt children from their
6 own countries; others adopt children from foreign countries. Some people adopt
7 children of their same race, i.e., white, black, Asian; others adopt children of
8 different races. In any case, they all adopt children for the same reason: they care
9 about children, and want to give their adopted child a happy life. This includes a
10 comfortable home, a loving family, and a good education.
11   Most adopted children know that they are adopted. Psychologists and
12 child care experts generally think this is a good idea. However, many adopted
13 children, or adoptees, have very little information about their biological mother
14 and father. As a matter of fact, it is often very difficult for adoptees to find out
15 about their birth parents because the birth records of most adoptees are usually
16 sealed. The information is confidential, so no one can see it. Sealed documents
17 protect both adoptees and their natural parents.

18 Naturally, adopted children have different feelings about their birth parents.
19 Many adoptees want to search for them, but others do not. Jake, who is thirteen,
20 was adopted when he was only two and a half months old. He says, "I don't
21 think I'll ever search out my birth mother. I might want to get some more facts,
22 but I don't feel I really want to go looking. Maybe she would be awful and I'd
23 just be disappointed." Carla, who is twelve, was adopted when she was four
24 years old. Her adoptive parents also adopted another little girl. Carla says,
25 "Sometimes my sister and I will talk. She says she doesn't want to look for
26 her birth mother when she gets older, but I have mixed feelings. Sometimes I
27 feel that I want to look for her—and my mother says she'll help me when I'm
28 older—but sometimes I don't want to look for her at all because I'm scared of
29 finding out what her reactions would be. I worry that she'll have a whole new
30 life and I'll just be interfering with that new life. She might not want anyone
31 to know about her past." Sue, who is thirteen, was adopted when she was a
32 baby. Her family helped her find her birth mother. Sue says, "I think adopted
33 kids should be allowed to search whenever they're ready. They need to know
34 where they came from. And they need to know what their medical history is.
35 As soon as I searched and found the information I was looking for, I felt more
36 worthwhile in the world. Beforehand, a part of me had always been missing."

37   The decision to search for birth parents is a difficult one to make. Most
38 adoptees, like Carla, have mixed feelings about finding their biological parents.
39 Even though adoptees do not know about their past or their natural parents, they
40 *do* know that their adoptive parents want them, love them, and will care for them.

Fact-Finding Exercise

Read the passage once. Then read the following statements. Check whether they are True or False. If the statement is false, rewrite the statement so that it is true. Then go back to the passage and find the line that supports your answer.

1 _____ True _____ False   Adoption is common in the United States.

_____

_____

_____

2 _____ True _____ False   People only adopt babies of their same race.

_____

_____

_____

3 _____ True _____ False   Most adopted children don't know they are adopted.

_____

_____

_____

4 _____ True _____ False   It is easy for adopted children to find their birth parents.

_____

_____

_____

5 _____ True _____ False   Most adoption birth records are confidential.

_____

_____

_____

6 _____ True _____ False   Jake wants to find his birth mother.

_____

_____

_____

7 _____ True _____ False   Sue found her birth mother.

_____

_____

_____

B

Skimming and Scanning Exercise

PART 1

Skim through the passage. Then read the following statements. Choose the one that is the correct main idea of the reading.

a. Most adopted children know they are adopted, but not all of them want to find their natural parents.
b. Some couples adopt children when they cannot have children of their own.
c. People adopt children of different ages, races, and from different countries.

Scan the passage. Work with a partner to fill in the chart below with information from the reading.

FEELINGS ABOUT ADOPTION		
Name	Do these children think it is a good idea to find birth parents?	Reasons
Childcare Experts	Yes / No / I don't know	
Jake	Yes / No / I don't know	
Carla	Yes / No / I don't know	
Sue	Yes / No / I don't know	

C

Reading Analysis

Read each question carefully. Circle the letter or the number of the correct answer, or write your answer on the blank line.

1 When couples get married, they usually plan to have children. Sometimes, however, a couple cannot have a child of their own. **In this case,** they may decide to adopt a child. **In fact,** adoption is very common today. There are **about 130,000** adoptions in the United States alone.

   a. **In this case** means
      1. when a couple cannot have children
      2. when a couple plans to have children
      3. when a couple gets married

b. What follows **in fact?**

    1. An example of adoption
    2. More information about adoption
    3. The reason for adoption

c. The last sentence means that

    1. the United States is the only country in the world where people adopt children
    2. about 130,000 adoptions take place in the United States, and many adoptions take place in other countries, too
    3. people who adopt children in the United States are alone

d. What does **about 130,000** mean?

    1. More than 130,000
    2. Less than 130,000
    3. Around 130,000

2 Some people prefer to adopt **infants;** others adopt older children. What is an **infant?**

    a. A very young baby
    b. A small child
    c. A young child

3 Some people adopt children of their same race, **e.g.,** white, black, Asian; others adopt children of different races. **In any case,** they all adopt children for the same reason: they care about children, and want to give their adopted child a happy life. **This** includes a comfortable home, a loving family, and a good education.

    a. What does **e.g.** mean?

        1. For example
        2. The same race
        3. Also

    b. What does **in any case** mean?

        1. When people adopt children of the same race
        2. It does not matter what kind of child they adopt
        3. If they adopt a child of a different race

    c. What information follows the colon (**:**)?

      1. An example
      2. An opposite idea
      3. A reason

    d. What does **this** refer to?

      1. A good education
      2. A happy life
      3. A loving family

4 Most adopted children know that they are adopted. Psychologists and child care experts generally think **this** is a good idea.

This refers to the fact that

    a. children know they are adopted
    b. people want to adopt children

5 Many adopted children, or **adoptees,** have very little information about their **biological mother and father. As a matter of fact,** it is often very difficult for adoptees to find out about their birth parents because the birth **records** of most adoptees are usually **sealed.** The information is **confidential,** so no one can see it. Sealed documents protect both adoptees and their natural parents.

    a. What does **adoptees** mean?

      1. Children who are adopted
      2. People who adopt children

    b. In this paragraph, what are synonyms for the words **biological mother and father?**

    _____

    c. What information follows **as a matter of fact?**

      1. More information about the same idea
      2. Different information about the previous idea

    d. Read the following sentence and complete it. The weather today is very cold. As a matter of fact,

      1. tomorrow will be cold, too
      2. the temperature is below freezing

e. Which word in this paragraph is a synonym for **records?**

_____

f. What are **sealed** documents?

1. They are documents that are in an envelope.
2. They are documents that no one can read.

g. What does **confidential** mean?

1. Important
2. Serious
3. Secret

6 **Naturally,** adopted children have different feelings about their birth parents. Many adoptees want to search for them, but others **do not.**

a. **Naturally** means

1. of course
2. however

b. What does **do not** mean?

1. Other adoptees do not want to search for their birth parents.
2. Other adoptees do not have different feelings about their birth parents.

7 Carla says, "My sister says she doesn't want to look for her birth mother, but I have **mixed feelings.** Sometimes I feel that I want to look for her— and my mother says she'll help me when I'm older—but sometimes I don't want to look for her because I'm scared of finding out what her reactions would be."

a. Why does Carla say that she has **mixed feelings?**

1. She does not want to look for her natural mother.
2. She wants to look for her natural mother.
3. She is not sure what she wants to do.

b. When you have **mixed feelings,** you

1. think two opposite ways about something
2. think differently from another person

8 Sue says, "Adopted kids need to know where they came from, and they need to know what their medical history is. As soon as I searched and found the information I was looking for, I felt more **worthwhile** in the world. **Beforehand,** a part of me had always been missing."

a. **Worthwhile** means

   1. unsure
   2. happy
   3. important

b. **Beforehand** refers to the time

   1. before something happens
   2. after something happens

c. Jack was on time when he arrived at the station to take the train. **Beforehand,**

   1. he went to bed early last night
   2. he had called the station to find out the train schedule

9 **Even though** adoptees do not know about their past or their natural parents, they *do* know that their adoptive parents want them, love them, and will care for them.

a. What does **even though** mean?

   1. Also
   2. Although
   3. However

b. Complete the following sentence. Even though the train was late,

   1. Karen arrived at work on time
   2. Karen was late to work

c. Why is **do** before the verb, and why is it in italics?

   1. To show emphasis
   2. To ask a question

Dictionary Skills

Read the dictionary entry for each word, and think about the context of the sentence. Write the number of the appropriate definition on the line next to the word. Then choose the sentence with the correct answer.

1

> **care** *v.* **cared, caring, cares** **1** [I; T] to worry about the well-being of others: *She cares about everyone; she is interested in and concerned about people.* || *He doesn't care about anyone but himself.* **2** [I; T] to be concerned about s.t.: *She cares about the quality of her work.* || *I really want to buy that car; I don't care if it costs too much!* **3 not to care for:** not to like or love: (love) *I don't care for her.* || (like) *He doesn't care for carrots or beans.* **4** *phrasal v. insep.* [T] **to care for s.o.** or **s.t.:** to look after s.o.'s health: *When she was sick, he cared for her day and night.* **5 to not care less:** to not care at all: *He is such a bad manager; I could not care less if he leaves the company.*

People adopt children because they **care** about them, and want to give their adopted child a happy life.

a. care: _____
b. 1. People adopt children because they worry about them.
　　2. People adopt children because they are concerned about the children's well-being.
　　3. People adopt children because they want to look after the children's health.

2

> **record** *n.* **1** s.t. (usu. written) that proves that an event happened, including records of business transactions, scientific data, cultural, or other human activities: *The records of our business are kept in our computer and in printouts.* **2** the best time, distance, etc., in an athletic event: *She holds the world record for the 100-meter dash.* **3** a criminal's history of arrests and things he or she did wrong: *That thief has a long criminal record.* **4** a flat, black disk onto which a sound recording, esp. music, has been pressed: *He has a collection of Elvis Presley records from the 1950s.*

The birth **records** of most adoptees are usually sealed because the information is confidential.

a. record: _____
b. 1. Written information about an adoptee's birth is confidential.
　　2. The criminal history of an adoptee's birth is confidential.
　　3. Information about an adoptee's birth is written on a flat, black disk.

[C]—Countable (noun); [U]—Uncountable (noun); s.o.—someone, s.t.—something; (*syn.*)—synonym; *n.*—noun; *v.*—verb; I—Intransitive; T—Transitive

history *n.* -ies **1** [C; U] the study of past events (people, civilizations, etc.): *She studied European history at college.* **2** [C] past events, a written account of past events: *My family history is very interesting; I plan to write it all down some day.* || *She read a history of Peru.* **3** **that's history** or **past (ancient) history**: s.t. that is no longer important: *His bad behavior is past history; he's a good boy now.* **4** **to make history**: to do s.t. memorable, important

Sue says, "Adopted kids need to know where they came from, and they need to know what their medical **history** is."

a. **history:** _____
b. 1. Adopted children need to find written accounts of their medical records.
    2. Adopted children need to study their past.
    3. Adopted children make their own history.

Word Forms

PART 1

In English, the noun form and the verb form of some words are the same, for example, *visit (v.)*, *visit (n.)*. Complete each sentence with the correct form of the words on the left. In addition, indicate whether you are using the verb *(v.)* or the noun *(n.)* form of each word. **Write all the verbs in the simple present tense. They may be affirmative or negative. The nouns may be singular or plural.**

plan

1 Terry has several _____ for his career. For example,
                          (v., n.)

he _____ to move to another city and to work for
      (v., n.)

the government.

care

2 All parents give love and _____ to their children. In
                      (v., n.)

happy families, parents and children _____ about
                           (v., n.)

each other very much.

record

3 The Records Office at City Hall keeps all the _____
(v., n.)

of births, marriages, and deaths. However, the Records

Office _____ sales of property. The City Real Estate
(v., n.)

Office keeps all that information on file.

search

4 When I lose my car keys, I usually _____ for them in
(v., n.)

my pockets. Sometimes my _____ is not successful,
(v., n.)

so I look for my keys on the floor.

worry

5 Lee has many _____ about his family. They are
(v., n.)

very important to him. However, he _____ about
(v., n.)

unimportant matters.

PART 2

In English, there are several ways that verbs change to nouns. Some verbs become nouns by adding the suffix -ion, for example, *suggest (v.)*, *suggestion (n.)*. Complete each sentence with the correct form of the words on the left. **Write all the verbs in the simple present tense. They may be affirmative or negative. The nouns may be singular or plural.**

decide *(v.)*

decision *(n.)*

1 Fred generally _____ where to go on vacation

after he reads some travel books. As a matter of fact,

Fred makes all his _____ after he reads books

or magazines.

react *(v.)*   **2**   John _____ strongly when he is surprised. He never says anything, or shows any feelings. His _____ are not usually easy to see.

reaction *(n.)*

protect *(v.)*   **3**   An umbrella _____ you from the rain when the wind is blowing very hard. On rainy and windy days, a raincoat gives better _____ than an umbrella does.

protection *(n.)*

adopt *(v.)*   **4**   When a couple _____ a child, the entire family is usually very happy. Before the _____ takes place, the whole family usually discusses the decision together.

adoption *(n.)*

inform *(v.)*   **5**   The Registrar's Office _____ students when they are accepted to a college. The Office of Admissions mails this _____ to the students.

information *(n.)*

Word Partnership	Use *information* with:
adj.	**additional** information, **background** information, **important** information, **personal** information
v.	**find** information, **get** information, **have** information, **provide** information, **retrieve** information, **store** information, **want** information

Vocabulary in Context

adopted *(v.)*	even though	protected *(v.)*
confidential *(adj.)*	in fact	worthwhile *(adj.)*
decided *(v.)*	infants *(n.)*	

Read the following sentences. Complete each blank space with the correct word from the list above. Use each word only once.

1 _____ drink milk from a bottle. They cannot use a cup.

2 Mr. Lee is not a new teacher at this school. _____, he started teaching here 15 years ago.

3 All medical records are _____. Only your doctor can read them.

4 This class is very _____ because I am learning a lot of English here.

5 Cara came to school _____ she is sick.

6 Seat belts are very important in a car. Mine _____ me when I had an accident last year.

7 Carlos is looking for a new apartment, but there are many places to choose. Finally, he _____ to move to Bayside because it is near his school.

8 Mr. and Mrs. Stevens wanted to start a family. They couldn't have a baby, so they _____ a child from their country.

Think About It

Read the following questions and think about the answers. Write your answer below each question. Then compare your answers with those of your classmates.

1 What might be some reasons why some people adopt children from foreign countries?

_____

_____

_____

2 What might be some reasons why adoptees want or need to find information about their natural parents?

_____

_____

_____

H

Another Look

Read this adoptive mother's journal entry. Then answer the questions that follow.

Track 8

Diary of an Adoptive Mother

1   **January 1:** It has happened; I got a call today saying a little girl in Russia is now
2 my little girl. There is a lot of paperwork to do, and we have to travel to Russia to bring
3 her home, but now it is certain. I think I'll tell some close friends. Jason is so excited.
4 I haven't told Steven yet. How can I tell a seven-year-old that he has a sister who is
5 already five years old?
6   **January 10:** Today I received a picture of Katerina. The picture is small and not
7 very clear, but I look at it over and over again. I don't know anything else about her.
8 She has lived in an orphanage for most of her life. I wonder how I will talk to her. I don't
9 speak Russian, and she doesn't speak English.

February 1: Today I showed Katerina's picture to Steven. He is very happy and wants to tell all his friends about his new sister. I want to buy some clothes for Katerina, but I don't know her size. I haven't received any more information from the adoption agency, and I'm feeling a little worried.

February 16: Finally! Today we received good news! All the papers are ready and tomorrow we will go to Russia to bring Katerina home with us.

February 18: Today I met my daughter for the first time. She is very small, very thin, and very afraid. On the way home in the airplane, she slept most of the time. When she woke up, she cried. I am very nervous and hope that I can be a good mother to Katerina.

February 19: Steven met his sister this morning. Although Katerina was shy at first, soon she and Steven began to communicate in a mixture of Russian, English, and hand gestures. Steven and his sister get along well together. In fact, he is able to help her communicate with Jason and me. I am worried about how Katerina will be in school. Next week she will start kindergarten. How will she communicate with the other children? How will she understand her teacher?

March 21: Katerina looks much healthier now. She has gained weight, her hair is shiny, and her skin is clear. She loves to watch television with her brother, and she has learned to roller-skate. She is doing well in school, and her English gets better every day. Although she sometimes looks sad, and sometimes cries, most of the time she is happy. I think she is slowly getting used to her new life with us. After only three months, I can't imagine my life without her.

UNIT 2   FAMILY LIFE

Questions for Another Look

1. Who is the writer of this diary? _____

2. Who is Katerina?
   a. The adoptive mother
   b. The adoptive father
   c. The adopted child

3. Who is Jason?
   a. The adoptive mother
   b. The adoptive father
   c. The adopted child

4. Who is Steven?
   a. The adoptive father
   b. The writer's son
   c. The adopted child

5. In the last sentence of the story, the writer says, "After only three months, I can't imagine my life without her." What does this sentence mean?
   a. The writer is happy that she has adopted Katerina.
   b. The writer is not happy that she has adopted Katerina.

I Topics for Discussion and Writing

1. Is adoption common in your country? Why or why not?

2. Do you think it is a good idea for adoptees to search for their birth parents? Explain your answer.

3. Do you think it is a good idea for people to adopt children who are a different race? Explain your answer.

4. In your country, can anyone adopt a child? For example, can a single man adopt a child? Do you think it is a good idea for anyone—male, female, married or single—to adopt a child? Explain your answer.

5 People sometimes give up their children for adoption. Imagine that you are going to give up your child. Write a letter to your best friend and explain your reasons.

6 **Write in your journal.** Imagine that you are married, and you cannot have children of your own. Will you adopt children? If you will, why is it important for you to have children? If you won't, explain your reasons.

J

Follow-Up Activities

1 Look at the following charts. Read the sentences and questions that follow and fill in the answers.

Adoption by Age of Adoptees in the United States in 2002

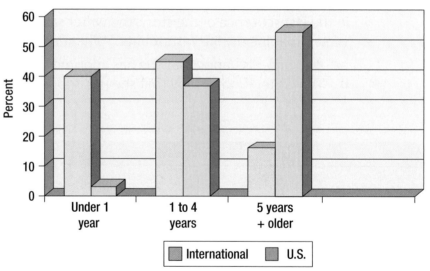

a. 1. Americans adopted _____ of babies under 1 year old from other countries.
   2. Americans adopted _____ of babies under 1 year old from the U.S.
   3. Americans adopted _____ of children 1-4 years old from other countries.
   4. Americans adopted _____ of children 5 years old and older from the U.S.

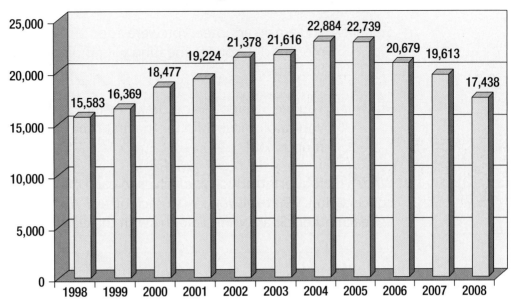

Adoptions to the United States

b. 1. Americans adopted _____ children from other countries in 2008.
    2. Americans adopted the most children from other countries in _____.
    3. Americans adopted the fewest children from other countries in _____.
    4. What are some reasons Americans adopt children from other
       countries? What do you think?

    _____

    _____

    _____

    _____

    _____

    _____

    _____

2 Work with another student.

Student A: You are an adoptee. You were adopted when you were six months old. You are meeting your biological mother for the first time.

Student B: You are Student A's natural mother/father. You are meeting your biological child for the first time since he/she was six months old.

Write a dialogue. Introduce yourselves to each other. Then have a conversation. What will you say to each other? What questions will you ask each other? Share your dialogue with the class.

_____

_____

_____

_____

_____

_____

_____

3 Work with a partner. Imagine that you want to adopt a child. What kind of child do you want? Describe the child's age, race, sex, and so on. Why do you want to adopt this particular kind of child? What kind of life do you want for your adopted child?

_____

_____

_____

_____

_____

_____

_____

_____

K

Word Search

Read the words listed below. Find them in the puzzle and circle them. They may be written in any direction.

adoption	decision	protect	sealed
care	history	react	search
confidential	information	record	worthwhile

```
L  J  R  Z  W  S  N  R  D  L  S  N  E  C  R
A  F  W  V  O  S  W  O  W  B  M  U  G  B  U
I  N  F  O  R  M  A  T  I  O  N  E  Q  R  R
T  H  I  S  T  O  R  Y  T  T  L  D  R  E  K
N  G  F  R  H  C  D  H  J  S  P  U  C  A  J
E  Z  C  U  W  D  E  C  I  S  I  O  N  C  C
D  E  R  B  H  M  S  T  R  W  R  A  D  T  N
I  S  K  P  I  K  T  D  O  D  S  L  J  A  M
F  S  E  A  L  E  D  Q  Y  R  V  Y  T  Y  I
N  G  R  A  E  P  U  J  E  A  P  T  Z  S  J
O  C  V  H  R  X  F  Z  W  L  V  V  R  B  Z
C  Z  H  Q  T  C  R  B  L  G  I  Q  F  S  M
C  B  K  Q  M  O  H  K  W  R  M  R  Z  J  D
```

Crossword Puzzle

Read the clues on the next page. Write the answers in the correct spaces in the puzzle.

UNIT 2   FAMILY LIFE

Crossword Puzzle Clues

1. I ate my food, and the dog ate _____ food.
5. _____ means make a child part of your family.
7. Response
8. I didn't eat anything all day. _____, I'm very hungry now.
12. The time before something happens
15. White, black, Asian: each one is a _____
16. At the present time
18. Adopted children
19. Closed; no one can see
21. Two people, usually a man and a woman
22. I have my books, and they have _____ books.
23. I didn't sleep well last night. I am _____ tired.

1. Babies
2. Make up your own mind about something
3. She likes her teacher. He likes _____ teacher, too.
4. Secret
6. We all have _____ own homes.
9. The opposite of **no**
10. Valuable
11. Look for
13. Biological mother and father
14. Records; important papers
17. She lost _____ bag.
20. You passed _____ test!
21. Parents _____ about their children.

Grammar Cloze Quiz

Read the passage. Complete each blank space with one of the pronouns listed in the box. You may use the pronouns more than once.

her	me	she	them
I	my	their	they

Naturally, adopted children have different feelings about _____ birth
(1)
parents. Many adoptees want to search for _____ , but others do not. _____
(2)   (3)
have different feelings. Jake says, " _____ don't think _____ will ever search
(4)   (5)
out _____ birth mother. _____ might want to get some more facts, but _____
(6)   (7)   (8)
don't feel _____ really want to go looking." Carla was adopted when _____
(9)   (10)
was four years old. _____ adoptive parents also adopted another little girl.
(11)
Carla says, "Sometimes _____ sister and _____ will talk. _____ says _____
(12)   (13)   (14)   (15)
doesn't want to look for _____ birth mother when _____ gets older, but _____
(16)   (17)   (18)
have mixed feelings. Sometimes _____ feel that _____ want to look for _____ ,
(19)   (20)   (21)
and _____ mother says _____ will help _____ when _____ am older."
(22)   (23)   (24)   (25)

| DISCUSSION

1. Some twins do not grow up together because they live with different
families. Sometimes these twins are adopted separately. Is this a good idea?
Explain your answer.

_____

_____

_____

2. Some families have adopted children in addition to their own biological children.
Do you think they are treated differently by the parents? Explain your answer.

_____

_____

_____

Technology in Our Everyday Lives

5
CHAPTER

Robots: The Face of the Future

Prereading Preparation

1 Look at the photograph. This is a robot called ASIMO. What do you think it can do? Make a list.

_____   _____

_____   _____

_____   _____

2 ASIMO looks like a person. Do you think all robots look like people? _____

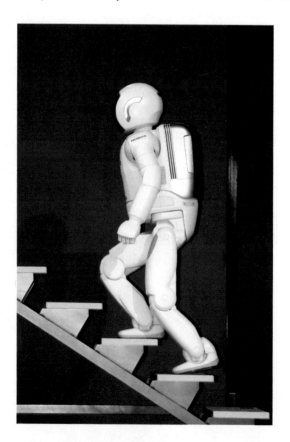

UNIT 3   TECHNOLOGY IN OUR EVERYDAY LIVES

3 Where do people use robots? Circle your answers. You can choose more than one answer.

    a. At home

    b. At work

    c. At school

4 Did you ever see a robot? Where did you see it? What did it do?

5 Imagine you have a robot. What do you want the robot to do for you? Make a list.

_____

_____

_____

_____

_____

Track 9

Robots: The Face of the Future

1   ASIMO traveled to Edinburgh, Scotland in February for the annual Edinburgh
2   International Science Festival. Thousands of people came to visit the festival, but
3   most of them came to see nine-year-old ASIMO. ASIMO is very famous because
4   ASIMO is a robot. It is designed to run, climb stairs, and kick a soccer ball. It can
5   even conduct an orchestra. In fact, when Yo Yo Ma, the famous cellist, performed
6   at a concert in Detroit, Michigan last year, ASIMO was the conductor. Everyone
7   at the concert was amazed not only by Yo Yo Ma but also by ASIMO.
8   A robot is not a new idea. Scientists developed robots more than 50 years ago.
9   For many years, robots have worked in factories. They do uninteresting jobs,
10   such as packaging food or assembling cars. They are often used to do dangerous
11   work as well. Most of these robots are shaped like machines; they do not look
12   like people. However, ASIMO looks like a person. In addition, it is equipped
13   with the ability to recognize and remember people.

14   While many countries are developing robots, Japan has the most robots of all.
15 It is also developing more robots very quickly. In Japan, 20 percent of the people
16 are over 65 years old. This means that a lot of Japanese people are senior citizens
17 who no longer work. Robots can do their work, and help take care of the senior
18 citizens, too. Japan hopes to have one million robots working in the country by
19 the year 2025. A single robot can replace, or do the work of, ten people!
20   Robots will become more useful and popular in the future. Right now you
21 can't buy a robot to do all your work, but you can buy one to help you around
22 the house. iRobot, an American company, announced that it has robots that
23 can wash, sweep, or vacuum your floor. Although these robots do not look like
24 people, they can work just as hard!

Fact-Finding Exercise

Read the passage once. Then read the following statements. Check whether
they are True or False. If a statement is false, rewrite the statement so that it is
true. Then go back to the passage and find the line that supports your answer.

1 _____ True _____ False   ASIMO can play the cello.

_____

2 _____ True _____ False Some robots do uninteresting and dangerous jobs.

_____

3 _____ True _____ False Most robots look like people.

_____

4 _____ True _____ False ASIMO has the ability to recognize people.

_____

5 _____ True _____ False Most people in Japan cannot work.

_____

6 _____ True _____ False One robot can do the work of ten people.

_____

7 _____ True _____ False Now you can buy a robot to wash your floor.

_____

B

Skimming and Scanning Exercise

PART 1

Skim through the passage. Then read the following statements. Choose the one that is the correct main idea of the reading.

    a. In the future, robots will do a lot of work for people.
    b. Twenty percent of the people in Japan are senior citizens.
    c. ASIMO can teach students and conduct an orchestra.

Scan the passage. Work with a partner to fill in the chart below with information from the reading.

Places Where People Use Robots	What Robots Can Do There
Home	
Factories	
Other Places	

C Reading Analysis

Read each question carefully. Circle the letter or the number of the correct answer.

1. Everyone at the concert was **amazed not only** by Yo Yo Ma **but also** by ASIMO.

   a. **Amazed** means

      1. confused
      2. surprised
      3. interested

   b. **Not only . . . but also** means

      1. however
      2. except
      3. and

c. Why were the people amazed by ASIMO?
1. It's a good conductor.
2. It can play the cello.
3. It's a robot.

2 Scientists **developed** robots more than 50 years ago. For many years, robots have worked in factories. They do jobs, such as **packaging** food.

a. **Developed** means
1. learned about
2. thought about
3. made

b. **Packaging** food is
1. making food for a company
2. carrying food to a truck
3. putting food into boxes

3 Most of these robots are **shaped** like machines; they do not look like people. However, ASIMO looks like a person. In addition, it is **equipped** with the ability to recognize and remember people.

a. **Shaped like** means
1. to have the same form
2. to be the same size

b. Which one of these is shaped like an egg? Circle your answer.

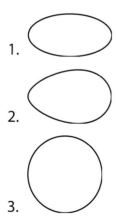

1.

2.

3.

c. **Equipped with** means
1. needs
2. makes
3. has

4 In Japan, 20 percent of the people are over 65 years old. This means that a lot of Japanese people are **senior citizens** who no longer work.

Senior **citizens** are people who

a. do not work
b. are 65 years old or older
c. have important jobs

5 Japan hopes to have 1 million robots working in the country by the year 2025. Does Japan have 1 million robots now?

a. Yes
b. No

6 A **single** robot can **replace,** or do the work of, ten people!

a. In this sentence, **single** means

1. not married
2. only one
3. new

b. In this sentence, **replace** means

1. one robot equals ten people at work.
2. ten robots equal one person at work.
3. one robot equals one person at work.

7 iRobot, an American company, **announced** that it has robots that can wash, sweep, or vacuum your floor.

Announced means

a. discovered
b. said
c. promised

8 These robots do not look like people, but they can work **just as hard!**

This sentence means

a. robots can work harder than people
b. people can work harder than robots
c. robots can do the same work as people

Dictionary Skills

Read the dictionary entry for each word and think about the context of the sentence. Write the number of the appropriate definition on the line next to the word. Then choose the sentence with the correct answer.

1

> **conduct** *n.* [U] **1** behavior, comportment: *Good conduct is expected of students in school.* **2** the process of doing s.t.: *the conduct of diplomacy* ‖ *the conduct of business*—*v.* **1** [T] to behave: *The students conducted themselves well in class today.* **2** [T] to do s.t.: *That store conducts business from 9:00 A.M. to 7:00 P.M.* **3** [I; T] to direct an orchestra, band, etc.: *He conducts the London Philharmonic Orchestra.*

ASIMO can even **conduct** an orchestra.

a. **conduct:** _____

b. 1. ASIMO can stand in front of an orchestra and direct its performance.
   2. ASIMO can do business for a musical performance.
   3. ASIMO can behave well during a musical performance.

2

> **assemble** *v.* -bled, -bling, -bles **1** [T] to put together, make: *The workers in that factory assemble trucks.* **2** [I] to gather, come together: *The crowd assembled in the meeting hall.*

They do uninteresting jobs, such as packaging food or **assembling** cars.

a. **assemble:** _____

b. 1. Robots come together in a group in a car factory.
   2. Robots are collected together in a car factory.
   3. Robots fit the parts of cars together in a factory.

3

> **recognize** *v.* [T] -nized, -nizing, -nizes **1** to recall, remember s.o. or s.t. when one sees or hears that person or thing: *I recognized an old friend in a crowd and waved to her.* **2** in a formal meeting, to give s.o. a chance to speak: *The chairwoman recognized me and I told the committee my opinion.* -*adv.* **recognizably**.

ASIMO is equipped with the ability to **recognize** and remember people.

a. **recognize:** _____

b. 1. ASIMO often speaks with people at meetings.
   2. ASIMO knows who a person is because it has seen that person before.
   3. ASIMO gives other people a chance to speak.

[C]—Countable (noun); [U]—Uncountable (noun); s.o.—someone, s.t.—something; *(syn.)*—synonym; *n.*—noun; *v.*—verb; I—Intransitive; T—Transitive

Word Forms

In English, some verbs become nouns by adding the suffix -ment, for example, *govern (v.), government (n.)*. Complete each sentence with the correct form of the word on the left. **Write all of the verbs in the past tense. The verbs may be affirmative or negative. The nouns may be singular or plural.**

amaze *(v.)*

amazement *(n.)*

1 The little girl looked in _____ at the animals on the farm. The cows, horses, sheep, and chickens _____ her because she lived in a city and never saw farm animals before.

develop *(v.)*

development *(n.)*

2 My new company _____ many advances in computer technology last year. Technological _____ are taking place there more and more quickly every year.

equip *(v.)*

equipment *(n.)*

3 Doctors need expensive _____ to conduct medical research. Last year, several research companies _____ their laboratories with millions of dollars worth of machines.

replace *(v.)*

replacement *(n.)*

4 Fifty years ago, robots _____ people at home, only in factories. Today, the _____ of people by robots at home for housework is becoming very common.

announce *(v.)*

announcement *(n.)*

5 When Roberto and Maria decided to get married, they happily _____ the news to their family and friends. They even put _____ in two of the local newspapers.

In English, the noun form and the verb form of some words are the same, for example, *visit (v.), visit (n.)*. Complete each sentence with the correct form of the words on the left. Then circle *(v.)* if you are using the verb, or *(n.)* if you are using a noun. **Write all of the verbs in the present tense. The verbs may be affirmative or negative. The nouns may be singular or plural.**

design

1 Jackie works for a clothing company. She _____
(v., n.)

women's dresses and suits. Her _____ are very
(v., n.)

fashionable.

package

2 The department store always _____ gifts in
(v., n.)

beautiful paper. Today is my birthday, and I received a gift

that came in a colorful _____ with a large bow
(v., n.)

and a card.

work

3 I _____ on weekends. My _____ is only
(v., n.)   (v., n.)

during weekdays, and never later than 5 P.M.

guide

4 We are not familiar with the city we are going to visit, so we

will get local _____ to show us the most interesting
(v., n.)

places. They often take tourists to places that are not in

tourist books. They _____ people around the city
(v., n.)

very well!

shape

5 These boxes come in a variety of _____, but not the
(v., n.)

one you need. Put your vase in paper. If you _____
(v., n.)

the paper to fit your vase, it won't break.

Word Partnership	Use *shape* with:
v.	**change** shape, **change the** shape **of something,** **get in** shape
adj.	**dark** shape, **(pretty) bad/good/great** shape, **better/worse** shape, **physical** shape, **terrible** shape

F Vocabulary in Context

amazed *(adj.)*	design *(v.)*	replace *(v.)*
announced *(v.)*	equipped *(adj.)*	senior citizens *(n.)*
assemble *(v.)*	recognize *(v.)*	

Read the following sentences. Complete each blank space with the correct word or phrase from the list above. Use each word or phrase only once.

1 The teacher _____ that we are going to have a grammar test
next week. I am going to begin studying this weekend.

2 My cell phone is broken. I will return it to the store and the store
will _____ it. I hope my new cell phone works better than
my old one!

3 Ann's new computer is _____ with a DVD player, speakers, and a camera.

4 Mickey bought a new bookcase. He must _____ it before he can use it.

5 My brother has a new haircut and looks very different. I almost didn't _____ him!

6 Clara is learning English very quickly. She is _____ at her fast progress.

7 Maryann really likes fashion, especially new clothes and shoes. She hopes to learn to _____ clothing in college.

8 Many _____ don't have to work any longer, so they have more time to spend with their grandchildren.

G Think About It

Read the following questions and think about the answers. Write your answers below each question. Then compare your answers with those of your classmates.

1 Most robots look like machines. They do not look like people. Is it important for robots to look like people? What do you think?

_____

_____

_____

_____

2 There are many senior citizens in Japan. In the future, robots will do their work and take care of senior citizens, too. How can robots take care of senior citizens?

_____

_____

_____

_____

_____

3 In many countries, including Japan, people must retire, or stop working, by a certain age, usually when they are 60 or 65 years old. This is a law. What is the reason for this law?

_____

_____

_____

_____

_____

4 iRobot has robots that can wash, sweep, and vacuum. What else do you want a robot to do for you in your home?

_____

_____

_____

_____

_____

Another Look

Read the following story about a new teacher in Japan. Then answer the questions that follow.

Track 10

An Unusual Teacher

1 Yuki Ishito's new 6th grade teacher, Sava, is like most teachers in Japan. This
2 morning, she is calling the attendance list, and asking the students in the back
3 of the room to "Please be quiet." Sava smiles at the students and looks happy.
4 "Thank you," she says. Sometimes she looks sad or angry. Other times, she can
5 look surprised or scared. Sava doesn't really look different from Yuki's other
6 teachers, but she is. Sava is a robot.
7   Hiroshi Kobayashi is a professor at the Tokyo University of Science. He
8 developed Sava. "Robots that look like people are a big hit with young
9 children," he said. Of course Sava cannot really teach the students. She is
10 remote-controlled by a person through a camera inside the robot.
11   Japan and other countries hope that in the future robots will do a lot of the
12 work that people do today. However, some scientists don't believe that a robot
13 can replace a teacher. Professor Kobayashi says, "Sava is just meant to help
14 people. The robot has no intelligence. It has no ability to learn. It's just a tool."
15 Although Sava is not ready to be a real teacher, the children enjoyed her visits.

Questions for Another Look

1 What can Sava do? Write three answers.

a. _____

b. _____

c. _____

2 "Robots that look like people are a big hit with young children." **A big hit** is an idiom. What does it mean?

   a. Famous

   b. Popular

   c. Effective

3 Do you think future robots can replace teachers? Why or why not?

_____

_____

_____

Topics for Discussion and Writing

1 Robots can do many different jobs. What jobs do you think robots **cannot** do? Why not? Talk about this with your classmates.

2 Robots do many dangerous or boring jobs. Robots also do interesting jobs. For example, ASIMO can conduct an orchestra. Will people be happy if robots do interesting jobs for them? Why or why not?

3 What are some of the advantages of having robots work in factories and other places, such as hospitals and homes for senior citizens? What are some of the disadvantages?

4 **Write in your journal.** Imagine that your teacher is a robot. Write a letter to a friend and describe your robot teacher. Tell your friend about your class. Do you enjoy your robot teacher? Why or why not?

J Follow-Up Activities

1 Work with a partner and design a new robot. What will it look like? What can it do?

_____

_____

_____

_____

2 Work in small groups. Pretend that you are the parents of children in a school. The school wants to replace a real teacher with a robot. You do not want your children to have a robot for a teacher. Give reasons why you think having a robot teacher is a bad idea.

_____

_____

_____

_____

3 Work in small groups. Pretend that you are the parents of children in a school. The school wants to replace a real teacher with a robot. You agree with this plan. Give reasons why you think having a robot teacher is a good idea.

_____

_____

_____

_____

4 Work in small groups. You manufacture robots that can teach children. Design an advertisement for your robot.

_____

_____

_____

_____

Word Search

Read the words listed below. Find them in the puzzle and circle them. They may be written in any directions.

amaze	develop	machine	scared
announce	equipped	replace	shape
design	famous	robot	surprised

```
L   E   C   N   U   O   N   N   A   M   W   B   Y   K   P
W   J   Q   M   S   W   V   T   D   E   V   E   L   O   P
O   L   P   Q   X   U   P   H   S   M   T   C   S   Z   S
K   K   Q   F   E   Z   R   U   C   Y   U   A   G   E   I
D   A   M   A   Z   E   B   P   A   G   U   L   L   W   K
F   A   M   O   U   S   N   G   R   J   U   P   Y   M   N
I   N   G   I   S   E   D   T   E   I   B   E   A   K   C
T   H   M   K   Q   H   E   M   D   C   S   R   N   L   F
O   U   M   Y   N   G   R   S   H   A   P   E   T   Y   O
B   M   P   Z   E   Q   U   I   P   P   E   D   D   L   F
O   G   U   S   O   G   E   N   I   H   C   A   M   T   I
R   Y   L   U   V   B   A   L   G   X   D   F   J   J   T
```

Crossword Puzzle

Read the clues on the next page. Write the answers in the correct spaces in the puzzle.

Crossword Puzzle Clues

1. The opposite of **down**
5. To lead musicians in a performance
6. The past tense of **is**
9. People over 65 are called _____ citizens.
10. These automobile _____ manufacture three different models of cars.
14. The airline company will make the _____ of a new airplane next week.
15. The opposite of **yes**
17. Put together
21. I _____ her. She's a student in my English class. Her name is Anna.
22. I, _____, **my**, **mine**
23. The opposite of **come**
24. **I**, **you**, _____, **she**, **it**, **we**, **they**
25. Some machines are _____ to do dangerous jobs.

2. Some people think that products have too much _____. They use too much paper.
3. A basketball, a baseball, and a soccer ball are all _____ like a sphere.
4. How much _____ do you need? Are these tools enough?
7. Scientists are working on the _____ of a machine that can do the work of many people.
8. _____, girl, man, woman
11. A musical performance
12. Susan loves her _____. She grows roses.
13. Will machines ever completely _____ teachers?
16. A machine that can do different kinds of work
18. One
19. Am, is, _____
20. My _____ is near the school. I'll give you my address.

Grammar Cloze Quiz

Read the passage. Complete each blank space with one of the prepositions listed below. You may use each preposition more than once.

by	in	of	over

A robot is not a new idea. Scientists developed robots more than 50 years ago. For many years, robots have worked _____ factories. They do
(1)
uninteresting jobs, such as packaging food or assembling cars. Most _____
(2)
these robots are shaped like machines; they do not look like people. However, ASIMO looks like a person. _____ addition, it is equipped with the ability
(3)
to recognize and remember people. While many countries are developing robots, Japan has the most robots _____ all. _____ Japan, 20 percent _____
(4)   (5)   (6)
the people are _____ 65 years old. This means that a lot _____ Japanese
(7)   (8)
people are senior citizens who no longer work. Robots can do their work, and help take care _____ the senior citizens, too. Japan hopes to have one
(9)
million robots working _____ the country _____ the year 2025. A single
(10)   (11)
robot can replace, or do the work _____, ten people!
(12)

CHAPTER 6

A New Way to Go

Prereading Preparation

Look at the photograph. This is a picture of a "Segway." Work with a partner and answer the questions below.

1. How many people can ride on it? _____

2. How fast do you think it goes? _____

3. Where can it be useful? _____

4. Who might it be useful for? _____

5. Why might it be useful? _____

6 How does the Segway get power?
   a. From an engine
   b. From batteries
   c. From the person riding on it

7 How much does a Segway cost? What do you think?
   a. $200
   b. $1,000
   c. $8,000

Track 11

A New Way to Go

1   It looks like a scooter, but it travels 15 miles per hour (24 kilometers per hour).
2   It uses two batteries and only ten cents of electricity a day. It can go backwards
3   or forwards, and it never falls over. It doesn't have brakes, but it knows when to
4   stop. What is it? It is a "Segway," and Dean Kamen invented it. It costs $8,000.
5   Right now, only a few people use the Segway scooter. This electric scooter
6   is very easy to use, and it can go in any direction. You can control it with your
7   body. For example, when you move to the left, the scooter moves to the left.
8   When you tilt forward, it goes straight ahead. In some states in the United States,
9   such as New Hampshire and Florida, post office workers use Segways to deliver
10 the mail. The scooters help the workers do their work more easily. In some cities,
11 such as Boston and Atlanta, police officers use them to travel on crowded streets.
12 Dean Kamen believes that many other people will soon ride Segways. The
13 scooters weigh about 65 pounds (about 29½ kilograms). They are cheaper than
14 cars, and they are faster than walking. Cars are useful for long distances. But
15 for short distances, electric scooters can be very useful. They are good for the
16 environment, too. They only use a little electricity and do not cause air pollution
17 like cars do. Dean Kamen believes that our lives will be a little easier with
18 his invention.

19 Before he invented the Segway, Dean Kamen worked on medical projects.
20 When his brother was in medical school, he needed an easier way to give
21 medicine to some patients. Dean's brother discussed this problem with him.
22 Dean invented a special machine so that patients do not have to take medicine
23 by mouth. Doctors can give them medicine through their skin. Now, many
24 doctors and hospitals use this machine.

25   In addition to the Segway, Dean Kamen has invented another device to make
26 life easier. It is a new kind of wheelchair to help people who cannot walk. This
27 wheelchair can climb curbs. It can "walk" up stairs, too. It can travel over rocks
28 and sand. This new wheelchair can even raise itself up so that the person in this
29 wheelchair can reach something on a high shelf. It can go up to the height of a
30 standing person.

31   Dean Kamen wants to help as many people as possible with his inventions,
32 and wants to encourage other people to invent useful devices, too.

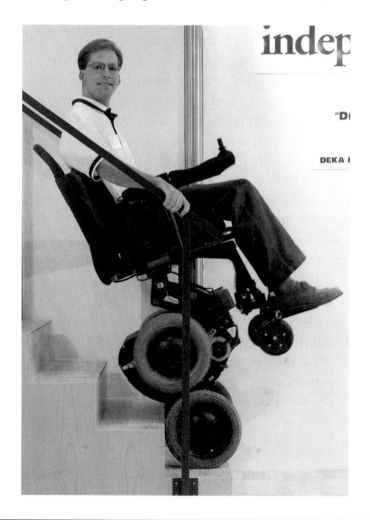

Fact-Finding Exercise

Read the passage once. Then read the following statements. Check whether they are True or False. If a statement is false, change the statement so that it is true. Then go back to the passage and find the line that supports your answer.

1 _____ True _____ False   The Segway uses a lot of electricity.

_____

2 _____ True _____ False   The scooter is helpful for postal workers and police officers.

_____

3 _____ True _____ False   Cars can cause air pollution.

_____

4 _____ True _____ False   Scooters can be useful for long distances.

_____

5 _____ True _____ False   Some doctors use Dean's other machine to give medicine to their patients.

_____

6 _____ True _____ False   The new wheelchair is helpful for postal workers and police officers.

_____

7 _____ True _____ False   The new wheelchair travels 15 miles per hour.

_____

Skimming and Scanning Exercise

Skim through the passage. Then read the following statements. Choose the one that is the correct main idea of the reading.

a. The new wheelchair can be very helpful because it climbs stairs and travels over rocks and sand.

b. Segways can be important to the environment because they do not cause air pollution.

c. Dean Kamen has invented many things that can make life easier for many different people.

PART 2

Scan the passage. Work with a partner to complete the chart.

	Dean Kamen's Inventions	
What is the invention?	*Segway*	
Who is it helpful for?		
Why is it helpful?		

Reading Analysis

Read each question carefully. Either circle the letter or the number of the correct answer or write your answer in the space provided.

1 A Segway can go **backwards** or **forwards,** and it never falls over. **Backwards** and **forwards** are

   a. synonyms

   b. antonyms

   c. numbers

2 This electric scooter is very easy to use, and can go in any **direction.** You can control it with your body. For example, when you move to the left, the scooter moves to the left. When you tilt forward, it goes straight ahead.

   a. **Direction** means

      1. way

      2. speed

      3. road

   b. What directions can the electric scooter go?

   _____

3 Segways are cheaper than cars, and they are faster than walking.

   a. Cars are

      1. more expensive than Segways

      2. the same price as Segways

      3. less expensive than Segways

   b. Walking is

      1. faster than a Segway

      2. slower than a Segway

      3. easier than a Segway

4 Segways are good for the environment. Write two reasons.

   a. _____

   b. _____

5 Dean's brother needed an easier way to give medicine to some **patients.** Dean invented a special machine so that patients do not have to take medicine by mouth. Doctors can give them medicine through their skin.

    a. Patients are

        1. people who work in a hospital

        2. people who study to become doctors

        3. people who are sick in a hospital

    b. It is easier for patients to take medicine

        1. through their skin

        2. by mouth

6 The new wheelchairs can climb **curbs. Curbs** are on

    a. stairs

    b. streets

    c. sidewalks

7 Dean Kamen wants to help as many people as possible with his **inventions,** and wants to encourage other people to invent things, too. **Inventions** are things you

    a. make

    b. find

    c. ride

D Dictionary Skills

Read the dictionary entry for each word, and think about the context of the sentence. Write the number of the appropriate definition on the line next to the word. Then choose the sentence with the correct answer.

Dean Kamen has invented another **device** to make life easier. It is a new kind of wheelchair to help people who cannot walk. This wheelchair can climb curbs. It can "walk" up stairs, too. This new wheelchair can even raise itself up so that the person in this wheelchair can reach something on a high shelf. Dean Kamen wants to help as many people as possible with his inventions and wants to encourage other people to invent new **devices** that are **useful**, too.

1 | **device** *n.* **1** an electrical or mechanical machine: *The computer is an electronic device.* **2** a tool or implement: *An electric can opener is also a device.* **3** a trick or secret means to an end: *His outbursts of anger are just a device to move everyone's attention from his guilt.* **4** **to leave to one's own devices:** to leave s.o. alone without help or interference

a. **device:** _____
b. 1. Dean Kamen has invented another mechanical machine to make life easier.
   2. Dean Kamen has invented another trick to make life easier.

2 | **useful** *adj.* **1** helpful, handy: *Tools, such as a hammer and screwdriver, are useful when you want to fix something.* **2** valuable, worthwhile: *Her language skills make her a useful addition to our team.* -adv. **usefully**; -n. [U] **usefulness**.

a. **useful:** _____
b. 1. Dean Kamen wants other people to invent new devices that are helpful.
   2. Dean Kamen wants other people to invent new devices that are valuable.

E | Word Forms

PART 1

In English, the noun form and the verb form of some words are the same, for example, *move (v.), move (n.)*. Complete each sentence with the correct form of the word on the left. Then circle *(v.)* if you are using a verb, or *(n.)* if you are using a noun. **Write all the verbs in the simple present tense. They may be affirmative or negative. The nouns may be plural or singular.**

work

1 My sister _____ on Monday. She only goes to
            (v., n.)

her job on Saturdays and Sundays. My father does all his

_____ in the evening.
(v., n.)

travel

2 José _____ every year to visit his family in Mexico.
       (v., n.)

   _____ can be very expensive for a large family.
       (v., n.)

control

3 Postal workers _____ the Segways with their
                      (v., n.)

   bodies. The _____ of these electric scooters is easy
                   (v., n.)

   to learn.

help

4 Sometimes I need a little _____ with my homework.
                                  (v., n.)

   My older sister often _____ me when I ask her.
                              (v., n.)

cause

5 There are many different _____ of pollution.
                                 (v., n.)

   Segways are good for the environment because they

   _____ air pollution.
       (v., n.)

PART 2

In English, some verbs become nouns by adding the suffix -ion, for example,
act (v.), action (n.). Complete each sentence with the correct form of the
words on the left. **Write all verbs in the simple present tense. They may be
affirmative or negative. The nouns may be singular or plural.**

invent (v.)

invention (n.)

1 Dean Kamen's many _____ can be helpful for

   people. Some people _____ new products to make

   our lives easier.

pollute *(v.)*

pollution *(n.)*

2 Bicycles _____ the air of crowded cities. Today, many people are worried about air _____.

discuss *(v.)*

discussion *(n.)*

3 After we read a story in class, the teacher _____ it with the class. We had a very interesting _____ in class last week.

add *(v.)*

addition *(n.)*

4 Inventors _____ to the list of new inventions every year. Many of these wonderful _____ help people move about, live longer, and feel healthier.

direct *(v.)*

direction *(n.)*

5 Teachers _____ their students to read each question carefully on an exam. The students read the _____ carefully so they won't make mistakes.

Word Partnership	Use *direction* with:
adj.	**general** direction, **opposite** direction, **right** direction, **wrong** direction
n.	**sense of** direction
v.	**change** direction, **move in a** direction, **lack** direction, **take** direction

Vocabulary in Context

control *(v.)*	directions *(n.)*	invented *(v.)*	pollution *(n.)*
device *(n.)*	encourage *(v.)*	patients *(n.)*	uses *(n.)*

Read the following sentences. Complete each blank space with the correct word from the list above. Use each word only once.

1. My parents always _____ me to work hard because they want me to be successful.

2. My cell phone has many wonderful _____. I can make phone calls, take a photograph, create an address book, and listen to music.

3. We like to play video games. We _____ the game with a joystick.

4. Dr. Hu takes good care of her _____. She helps them to feel better very quickly.

5. Can you give me _____ to the library? I don't know where it is.

6. Alexander Graham Bell _____ the first telephone in 1878.

7. An answering machine is a _____ that records telephone messages when you are not at home and cannot answer the phone.

8. I like to ride my bicycle to school. It's good exercise, and it doesn't cause air _____.

Think About It

Read the following questions and think about the answers. Write your answers below each question. Then compare your answers with those of your classmates.

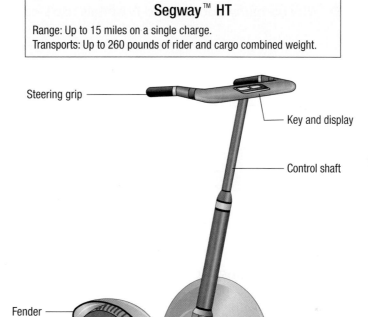

Segway™ HT

Range: Up to 15 miles on a single charge.
Transports: Up to 260 pounds of rider and cargo combined weight.

Steering grip

Key and display

Control shaft

Fender

Battery pack

Tire

Wheel

Rider detection system /
motor / batteries

1 Why don't many people have Segways?

_____

_____

_____

2 Why is it important that the new wheelchairs reach the height of a standing person?

_____

_____

_____

3 Why do many doctors and hospitals use Dean Kamen's medical invention?

_____

_____

_____

Another Look

Read the following information about organizations that encourage young inventors. Then answer the questions that follow.

Track 12

Young Inventors

1 Many organizations have contests to encourage young people to use their
2 imaginations and make new inventions. The winners of the competitions
3 receive prizes, usually money or scholarships for college. For example, last year,
4 12-year-old Jonathan Edwards was one of the winners of the Young Inventors'
5 Contest. This competition encourages students in elementary schools to use their
6 imagination. Jonathan invented the Step Ramp. The Step Ramp is stairs that
7 flatten down into a ramp. This special ramp can help people move heavy objects
8 up the stairs. It can also be very useful for people in wheelchairs.

Ryan Patterson, who is 18 years old, won a $100,000 scholarship in the Westinghouse Science and Technology contest for his useful invention. It is a special glove, called the Sign Language Translator. People who are deaf and cannot speak sometimes use sign language. They use their hands to "speak." When they wear Ryan's special glove, it translates sign language into words on a small computer screen. He hopes that his Sign Language Translator will be helpful and easy for many people to use.

Some contests also encourage young people to find ways to save energy. Every year, the U.S. Department of Energy has an "Energy Smart Schools" contest. Students can use their imaginations and their science knowledge. Michael Torrey, a fifth grader, invented a Miniature Hydroelectric Power Plant. This small device goes inside water pipes. Then the device uses water to charge batteries, such as the batteries in a small radio. While someone is taking a shower or brushing their teeth, for example, the running water charges the batteries.

Jonathan Ioviero is a fifth grader, too. He invented the "Light Searcher." This device "looks" around the house. It can find lights that are on in empty rooms. Then it can turn the lights off. Both Michael's and Jonathan's devices are useful because they can help save energy. These young inventors can help people and the environment at the same time!

Questions for Another Look

1. Use the information in the story to complete the chart.

Inventor's Name	Invention	What does it do?	Who can use it?

2. Which invention is the most useful? Why do you think so?

_____

_____

_____

Topics for Discussion and Writing

1. In what other places do you think electric scooters can be helpful? Why?

2. What do you think was the most important invention in the past? Why was this invention important? Write some reasons, and give examples.

3. What do you think might be an important invention in the future? Write about it. Describe what it might do and whom it might help.

4. **Write in your journal.** Think of a new invention that people need today. What will it do? Why will it be important? Who will be able to use it? How much might it cost?

Follow-Up Activities

1 Postal workers and police officers in some cities use Segways because they are helpful. Work in small groups. These electric scooters might be useful for other people, too. Make a list of these people, and write a reason why these scooters might be useful for them.

_____

_____

_____

2 Work in a group. Think of an invention that people need. Describe your invention. Draw a picture of it if you can. Explain to the class why this invention is necessary or useful.

_____

_____

_____

Word Search

Read the words listed below. Find them in the puzzle and circle them. They may be written in any direction.

climb	deliver	encourage	pollution
control	direction	invention	scooter
crowded	electricity	machine	wheelchair

```
E  N  F  E  Q  Y  Z  C  A  X  B  C  M  G  Z
N  L  T  X  R  U  O  I  I  I  G  R  Z  Z  Y
N  A  E  C  J  N  T  N  D  E  L  I  V  E  R
Z  O  K  C  T  H  V  W  H  P  I  W  A  C  O
M  R  I  R  T  E  H  N  R  C  X  H  G  I  G
A  C  O  T  N  R  N  O  I  T  C  E  R  I  D
C  L  R  T  U  N  I  L  T  C  T  E  E  T  F
H  U  I  O  S  L  A  C  F  Q  C  L  G  M  C
I  O  H  J  W  E  L  R  I  Y  L  C  A  D  L
N  O  K  Y  B  D  E  O  W  T  H  H  R  E  D
E  M  B  G  S  T  E  L  P  I  Y  A  U  E  F
M  W  B  N  O  D  S  D  G  W  M  I  O  O  K
O  X  A  O  C  J  D  Q  J  L  S  R  C  U  R
O  J  C  B  M  I  L  C  W  G  L  C  N  A  L
K  S  X  Q  K  G  N  Q  C  K  S  O  E  L  I
```

Crossword Puzzle

Read the clues on the next page. Write the answers in the correct spaces in the puzzle.

Crossword Puzzle Clues

3. A place to buy stamps (2 words)
4. Not easy
5. The opposite of **forwards**
8. Create something new
9. The place where you go to learn
10. Lift something up
12. Everything around us
13. Helpful
16. Talk about
18. Sick people in a hospital

1. The opposite of **right**
2. This causes dirty air or water.
4. People who give medicine
5. We use these to stop a car.
6. Boston and Atlanta
7. People who protect us
11. New Hampshire and Florida
14. $29\frac{1}{2}$ kg = 65 _____
15. Not expensive
17. This covers your whole body.

Grammar Cloze Quiz

Read the passage. Complete each blank space with one of the prepositions listed below. You may use the prepositions more than once.

by	on	through	up
in	over	to	with

Before he invented the Segway, Dean Kamen worked on medical projects. When his brother was _____ (1) medical school, he needed an easier way to give medicine _____ (2) some patients. Dean's brother discussed this problem _____ (3) him. Dean invented a special machine so that patients do not have to take medicine _____ (4) mouth. Doctors can give them medicine _____ (5) their skin. Now many doctors and hospitals use this machine.

In addition to the Segway, Dean Kamen has invented another device to make life easier. It is a new kind of wheelchair. It can climb curbs and "walk" _____ (6) stairs, too. It can travel _____ (7) rocks and sand. This new wheelchair can even raise itself _____ (8) so that the person in this wheelchair can reach something _____ (9) a high shelf. It can go _____ (10) to the height of a standing person.

1. The two chapters in this unit describe many uses of modern technology and many technologically advanced products. In both chapters, computer technology is very important. How is computer technology important in our everyday lives?

_____

_____

_____

_____

_____

2. Technology is an important part of our lives today. What are the advantages of modern technology? What are the disadvantages?

_____

_____

_____

_____

_____

Healthy Living

7

CHAPTER

Improving Lives with Pet Therapy

Prereading Preparation

1 Work with one or two partners. Fill in the chart below. When you are finished, compare your responses with those of your classmates.

Problems	Solutions
What do you do when you feel lonely?	
What do you do when you feel stressed?	
What do you do when you feel sick?	

2 Take a survey in the class. How many students like dogs? Why? How many students like cats? Why?

Number of Students Who Like Dogs	Reasons Why Students Like Dogs	Number of Students Who Like Cats	Reasons Why Students Like Cats

3 There are approximately 68 million dogs in homes in the United States, and approximately 73 million cats. Why do you think Americans have so many of these pets in their homes?

_____

_____

4 Read the title of the chapter. How can pets improve our lives? Make a list.

_____   _____

_____   _____

Track 13

Improving Lives with Pet Therapy

1   Do you sometimes feel lonely? Do you sometimes feel stressed? Do you
2   sometimes feel sick? If you answered "Yes" to these questions, you might not
3   need a doctor. Instead, you might just need a pet. Pets, like dogs, cats, or even
4   birds, can make you feel better. In fact, many people feel healthy when they have
5   a pet to take care of.
6   People who have pets often feel calmer and less lonely than people who don't
7   have pets. For example, Juliet Locke has a six-year-old cat named Snowball.
8   "Snowball knows when I'm having a bad day. When I'm sitting in a chair, she'll
9   jump on my lap and I'll pet her. She really helps me feel relaxed," says Juliet.
10 Pets can help you have a healthy mind, and they can give you a healthy body,
11 too. Dr. R.K. Anderson is a veterinarian. He started CENSHARE (Center to

12 Study Human/Animal Relationships and Environments), an organization that
13 researches how pets affect people. These researchers believe that people with pets
14 are healthier than people without pets. For instance, pet owners often have low
15 rates of heart disease. Many pet owners don't have high blood pressure, either.
16 While most people think of dogs and cats as pets, having birds and fish can also
17 be effective. In fact, people own many different kinds of pets. Researchers studied
18 the effects of these kinds of animals on their owners' health. The researchers
19 found that some people actually lower their blood pressure by watching fish in
20 a tank, or by listening to the sounds of birds. These activities are very calming.

21 Richard Waxman believes that all people should have the chance to spend
22 time with a pet. He started a group called "Paws and Hearts." It is a volunteer
23 organization that brings animals to nursing homes, hospitals and senior centers.
24 Mr. Waxman says that each patient can become friends with a loving dog. As a
25 result, the patients feel calmer, and also have less physical pain. This is called
26 "pet therapy," and people love the animals' visits. For example, Clara Wu lives
27 at a nursing home in Palm Desert, California. "I just love when the volunteers
28 bring the dogs to visit us," Mrs. Wu says. "It brings back wonderful memories
29 of other dogs I've owned." Mr. Waxman agrees. "Pet therapy allows for a great
30 connection between the past and the present that can be very powerful."

31 Paws and Hearts isn't only for adults. The organization also has a reading
32 program for children called "Paws to Read." Volunteers bring dogs to schools
33 and libraries. There, children sit with the dogs and read stories to them.
34 This activity often improves the children's reading skills as well as their
35 self-confidence. Then when they return to their classrooms, they feel more sure
36 of themselves and can read aloud more easily and clearly. It's easy to see that pet
37 therapy is useful for people of all ages.

Fact-Finding Exercise

Read the passage once. Then read the following statements. Check whether they are True or False. If a statement is false, rewrite the statement so that it is true. Then go back to the passage and find the line that supports your answer.

1 _____ True _____ False People who have pets often feel less healthy than people who don't have pets.

_____

2 _____ True _____ False Snowball is a six-year-old dog.

_____

3 _____ True _____ False People sometimes feel calm by watching fish in a tank or by listening to the sounds of birds.

_____

4 _____ True _____ False Patients at a nursing home in Palm Desert, California, are happy when the pets come to visit them.

_____

5 _____ True _____ False Volunteers from "Paws to Read" bring dogs to nursing homes and hospitals.

_____

6 _____ True _____ False The children's reading skills often improve by reading stories to the dogs.

_____

Skimming and Scanning Exercise

Skim through the passage. Then read the following statements. Choose the one that is the correct main idea of the reading.

    a. People in hospitals feel healthier when pets visit them.
    b. Pets can be very helpful to people.
    c. People of all ages enjoy pets.

PART 2

The story describes three groups or organizations. Scan the passage. Work with a partner to fill in the chart with information about the groups from the reading.

What is the name of the group or organization?	What is the group's purpose?	What is the result of the group's work?
1.		
2.		
3.		

C

Reading Analysis

Read each question carefully. Either circle the letter or the number of the correct answer or write your answer in the space provided.

  1 Do you sometimes feel lonely? Do you sometimes feel stressed? Do you sometimes feel sick? If you answered "Yes" to these questions, you might not need a doctor. **Instead,** you might just need a **pet.** Pets, like dogs, cats, or even birds, can help you feel better. **In fact,** many people feel healthy when they have a pet to take care of.

a. **Instead** means

   1. in place of
   2. in addition to
   3. together with

b. A **pet** is

   1. an animal you keep in your home
   2. a dog or a cat
   3. a bird

c. Which animals can make you feel better?

   1. Only dogs or cats
   2. Only birds
   3. Dogs, cats, birds, and other animals

d. What kind of information follows **in fact?**

   1. New, different information from the idea in the previous sentence
   2. More details about the idea in the previous sentence
   3. An example of the idea in the previous sentence

2 "Snowball knows when I'm having **a bad day.** When I'm sitting in a chair, she'll jump on my **lap** and I'll pet her. She really helps me feel relaxed," says Juliet.

a. **A bad day** means

   1. an unhappy or stressful day
   2. a day with bad weather
   3. an unlucky day

b. Someone's **lap** is

   1. the chair a person is sitting on
   2. the top of your legs when you are sitting down
   3. a small table

3 Researchers believe that people with pets are healthier than people without pets. **For instance,** pet owners often have low rates of heart disease. Many **pet owners** don't have high blood pressure, either. While most people think of dogs and cats as pets, birds and fish can also be effective. In fact, people **own** many different kinds of pets.

a. What does **for instance** mean?

   1. However
   2. For example
   3. Of course

b. A **pet owner** is someone who
  1. has a pet at home
  2. likes animals
  3. has high blood pressure

c. How are people with pets healthier than people without pets?
  1. They often have low rates of heart disease
  2. They typically don't have high blood pressure
  3. Both 1 and 2

d. Which animals can be helpful in making people healthier?
  1. Dogs
  2. Cats
  3. Birds
  4. Fish
  5. All of the above

4 Volunteers bring dogs to schools and libraries. **There,** children sit with the dogs and read stories to them. This activity helps to improve the children's reading skills as well as their **self-confidence.** Then when they return to their classrooms, they feel more sure of themselves and can read **aloud** more easily and clearly.

a. **There** refers to
  1. in schools and libraries
  2. only in schools
  3. only in libraries

b. When you read **aloud,** you read
  1. silently, without speaking
  2. quietly to yourself
  3. so that others can hear you

c. What group of words in these sentences is a synonym for **self-confidence?**

_____

D Dictionary Skills

Read the dictionary entry for each word and think about the context of the sentence. Write the number of the appropriate definition on the line next to the word. Then choose the sentence with the correct answer.

1 | **effective** *adj.* **1** having the result that one wants, productive: *The medication is quite effective; it relieves pain quickly.* **2** in use, current: *The law was effective on January 1. -adv.* **effectively;** *-n.* [U] **effectiveness.**

Many pet owners don't have high blood pressure, either. While most people think of dogs and cats as pets, having birds and fish can also be **effective.**

a. **effective:** _____
b. 1. Having pets is a law.
   2. Having pets makes no difference to people's health.
   3. Having pets can help people be healthier.

2 | **relax** *v.* -es **1** [I; T] to stop work and enjoy oneself: *She relaxes by riding her bicycle.* **2** [I; T] to stop being nervous, tense, angry, etc.: *Why don't you stop being angry and relax for a while!* **3** [T] to become or make weaker, looser, less strict: *Our dress code about what we should wear to work is relaxed in the summer.*

"Snowball knows when I'm having a bad day. When I'm sitting in a chair, she'll jump on my lap and I'll pet her. She really helps me feel **relaxed**," says Juliet.

a. **relax:** _____
b. 1. A pet makes people leave work.
   2. A pet makes people feel less worried.
   3. A pet makes people feel weak.

3 | **therapy** *n.* [U] treatment of mental and physical illnesses and disorders, usu. without surgery, such as speech therapy, physical therapy, etc.: *She began therapy to overcome her fear of crowds.*

Mr. Waxman says that each patient can become friends with a loving dog. As a result, the patients feel calmer, and also have less physical pain. This is called "pet **therapy**," and people love the animals' visits.

a. **therapy:** _____
b. 1. Patients and their pets have surgery so they feel better.
   2. Patients feel better after discussing their problems with a pet.
   3. Patients begin to feel better after becoming friends with a pet.

Word Forms

In English, some nouns become adjectives by adding the suffix *-ful*, for example, *hope (n.)*, *hopeful (adj.)*. Complete each sentence with the correct form of the word on the left.

stress *(n.)*

stressful *(adj.)*

1 Being a police officer is a very _____ job. In fact, police officers experience so much _____ that they often leave their jobs before they retire.

pain *(n.)*

painful *(adj.)*

2 Having a toothache can be extremely _____. If you have severe _____ in one of your teeth, you should visit a dentist as soon as possible.

help *(n.)*

helpful *(adj.)*

3 Thank you for your offer, but I don't need any _____ with my math homework. The explanations in my textbook are very clear and _____ to me.

power *(n.)*

powerful *(adj.)*

4 In the past, kings and queens were very _____ people. Today, however, kings and queens in most countries have very little _____. They no longer have complete control of their countries.

use *(n.)*

useful *(adj.)*

5 In the 21st century, people have less and less _____ for CDs. MP3 players seem to be much more _____ to them.

In English, the noun form and the verb form of some words are the same, for example, *cause (v.), cause (n.).* Complete each sentence with the correct form of the words on the left. Then circle *(v.)* if you are using a verb, or *(n.)* if you are using a noun. **Write all of the verbs in the present tense. The verbs may be affirmative or negative. The nouns may be singular or plural.**

answer

1 Mark always ＿＿＿＿＿＿ his friends quickly when they
(v., n.)

text-message him because he doesn't like to keep them

waiting for his ＿＿＿＿＿＿.
(v., n.)

volunteer

2 Arthur and Linda are ＿＿＿＿＿＿ at a children's hospital.
(v., n.)

They ＿＿＿＿＿＿ at a senior center, because they only
(v., n.)

like to work with children.

visit

3 Sarah loves her grandparents' ＿＿＿＿＿＿ from out of
(v., n.)

town. They often ＿＿＿＿＿＿ on holidays, and always on
(v., n.)

Sarah's birthday!

need

4 People who live in a desert have a serious ＿＿＿＿＿＿ for
(v., n.)

fresh water. They ＿＿＿＿＿＿ anything else if they have
(v., n.)

enough water. They usually have enough food.

return   **5** I never worry when my dog runs away because he usually

_____ before dark. His _____ home is
      (v., n.)   *(v., n.)*

always very welcome.

Word Partnership	Use *return* with:
v.	**decide to** return, **plan to** return
n.	return **trip**
	return **a (phone) call**
	return **to work**

F Vocabulary in Context

aloud *(adv.)*	**instead** *(adv.)*	**stressful** *(adj.)*
effective *(adj.)*	**powerful** *(adj.)*	**therapy** *(n.)*
for instance	**self-confidence** *(n.)*	

Read the following sentences. Complete each blank space with the correct word from the list above. Use each word only once.

1 The teacher sometimes reads a story _____ to the class.

We always listen carefully.

2 Mariella enjoys reading as much as she can. _____, she reads

on the bus, during lunch, and before class, too.

3 I wanted a dog for a pet, but my parents said no, so I got

a cat _____.

4 I prefer to send email to my family. It's much more _____ than writing letters. It's faster and easier, too.

5 Sung Min plays the piano very well. He has a lot of _____ and is never afraid to perform for large groups of people.

6 Having a pet, listening to soft music, taking a warm bath, are all very effective kinds of _____. They all help us feel relaxed.

7 At first, it can be very _____ to go to a new school. However, students often feel calmer after the first week.

8 Doctors can give patients very _____ medicine for pain when aspirin isn't strong enough.

G

Think About It

1 Why do you think people who have pets often feel calmer and less lonely than people who don't have pets?

_____

_____

_____

2 Researchers say that pet owners often have low rates of heart disease. Many pet owners don't have high blood pressure either. What do you think are reasons for this?

_____

_____

_____

3　The reading talks about cats, dogs, birds, and fish as helpful pets. Which animal could be most effective for certain people? For example, which animal might be most helpful for a child? For an elderly person? For someone in a hospital?

_____

_____

_____

4　The reading talks about the usefulness of pets for the elderly and for children. What other people can pets help? How can they be helpful?

_____

_____

_____

Another Look

Read the following story about pet therapy at a university. Then answer the questions that follow.

Track 14

A New Way to Relieve Student Stress

1   It's the last week of the semester at the University of Wisconsin. The students
2 are preparing for their final exams. Of course, this is a very stressful week for
3 many of them. Some are at the library, but they are not studying. Instead, they
4 are sitting and relaxing with dogs, but they are not wasting their time. The
5 Health Department of the university brings the dogs to the school library for the
6 students. The dogs help them to feel less stress as they prepare for their finals.
7   Counselors from the school bring the dogs, but they also bring advice for
8 the students about how to feel less anxious. They advised the students to take
9 short study breaks – even five minutes every hour – to reduce stress. These
10 frequent breaks also help the students to remember information. In addition, the
11 counselors advised the students to get enough sleep. "Don't drink a lot of coffee
12 because that will prevent you from sleeping," one counselor suggests. "Try not
13 to worry so much," another counselor says, "and ask your friends and family for
14 their assistance."
15   Manuel Perez, a University of Wisconsin student, says that all of the advice is
16 very useful. However, he says, "The dogs are the most useful of all. When I'm
17 petting one, I feel much more relaxed and then I'm ready to hit the books."

Questions for Another Look

1 Why is this a stressful week for the students?

_____

2 How do the dogs help the students?

_____

3 What advice did the counselor give the students to feel less stress?

a. _____

b. _____

c. _____

4 "I'm ready **to hit the books**" is an idiom. This means:
a. I'm ready to study.
b. I dropped my books.
c. I'm ready for the exam.

Topics for Discussion and Writing

1 Do you have a pet? Describe it. Explain why you enjoy your pet. If you don't have a pet, do you want to get one? Why or why not? Explain your answer.

2 How do you relax when you feel stressed? Write about what makes you calm.

3 Work in a small group. When you prepare for an important test, how do you study for it? Discuss what each of you does, and which is effective. Then write a letter to the other students. Give them advice to help them study effectively for a big exam.

4 **Write in your journal.** Write about a time when you felt a lot of stress. Why was it stressful? Explain your answer.

Follow-Up Activities

1 Read the following statistics about cats and dogs. Then read the sentences that follow. Fill in the blanks with the words **cat** or **dog**.

Dogs

- There are approximately 68 million dogs in homes in the United States.
- Four in ten (or 40 million) U.S. households own at least one dog.
- Most owners own one dog (63%).
- About one-fourth (24%) of owners own two dogs.
- On average, dog owners spent $196 on veterinary related expenses in the past 12 months.

Cats

- There are approximately 73 million cats in homes in the United States.
- Three in ten (or 34.7 million) U.S. households own at least one cat.
- One half of cat-owning households (49%) own one cat; the remaining (51%) own two or more.
- Cat owners spent an average of $104 on veterinary related expenses in the past 12 months.

a. There are more _____ owners than _____ owners in the U.S.

b. _____ owners spend more money on veterinary expenses

than _____ owners.

c. Most _____ owners have more than one.

d. Most _____ owners have only one.

2 Work alone or with a partner. Choose a pet you want to have. Find out what the pet needs, such as food, exercise, a place to sleep, training. How much will it cost to take care of this pet?

_____

_____

_____

K Word Search

Read the words listed below. Find them in the puzzle and circle them. They may be written in any direction.

activities	instead	patient	stressful
aloud	library	pets	useful
effective	lonely	powerful	veterinarian
healthy	lower	self-confidence	

```
S  Y  E  R  B  S  E  R  M  N  S  G  W  Y  I
Y  S  N  E  X  F  C  C  M  M  T  R  A  B  V
L  Y  R  W  I  E  N  V  D  V  R  E  C  C  E
W  U  Z  O  F  F  E  T  L  B  E  I  T  B  T
B  C  F  L  C  D  N  I  E  S  N  I  W  E
U  D  K  R  S  J  I  E  B  F  S  S  V  G  R
O  R  Y  G  E  R  F  I  R  F  F  T  I  P  I
O  L  L  K  K  W  N  T  A  E  U  E  T  H  N
U  S  E  F  U  L  O  A  R  C  L  A  I  E  A
E  W  N  Q  N  K  C  P  Y  T  E  D  E  A  R
F  E  O  F  Q  N  F  D  J  I  Z  M  S  L  I
I  M  L  G  C  H  L  S  U  V  M  C  F  T  A
C  E  Y  R  L  D  E  C  L  E  Z  Y  Z  H  N
J  S  T  E  P  O  S  D  U  O  L  A  F  Y  M
```

146

UNIT 4   HEALTHY LIVING

Crossword Puzzle

Read the clues on the next page. Write the answers in the correct spaces in the puzzle.

Crossword Puzzle Clues

2. Aspirin is very _____. It works very well.
4. I don't have the _____ to your question.
5. Both children and _____ love pets.
7. Do you _____ an extra pen?
8. When you feel _____, you feel relaxed.
9. It is _____ cold today–below freezing!
10. Susan didn't sleep well. In _____, she only slept two hours last night.
12. The opposite of **down**
15. I feel a lot of _____ before I take a test.
17. High _____ pressure can be dangerous to your health.
20. Come back
21. To do work for no pay
24. That horse is _____. It can pull heavy things.
25. Harry's grandmother is in a _____ home.
27. I don't want coffee. I want tea _____.

1. Doctors do _____ to test their ideas.
3. For example; for_____
6. This book is _____. I get many ideas from it.
11. We _____ our parents every weekend. They live nearby.
13. My headache is very _____. It hurts a lot.
14. The opposite of **yes**
16. Pets visit libraries and _____ for the children.
18. The _____ of that dog loves it very much.
19. The past of **do**
22. Pet _____ helps adults and children.
23. The opposite of **sick**
25. He doesn't _____ a coat. It's warm outside.
26. A dog or a cat makes a good _____.
28. My dog wants to go out, _____ I am taking it for a walk.

Grammar Cloze Quiz

Read the passage. Complete each blank space with one of the prepositions listed below. You may use the prepositions more than once.

by	in	of	on	to

Pets, like dogs, cats, or even birds, can make you feel better. _____ fact, (1)
many people feel healthy when they have a pet _____ take care _____. Juliet (2) (3)
Locke has a six-year-old cat named Snowball. "Snowball knows when I'm
having a bad day. When I'm sitting _____ a chair, she'll jump _____ my lap (4) (5)
and I'll pet her. She really helps me feel relaxed," says Juliet. Researchers believe
that people with pets are healthier than people without pets. For instance, pet
owners often have low rates _____ heart disease. Many pet owners don't have (6)
high blood pressure, either. While most people think _____ dogs and cats as (7)
pets, having birds and fish can also be effective. Researchers studied the effects
of these kinds of animals _____ their owners' health. The researchers found (8)
that some people actually lower their blood pressure _____ watching (9)
fish _____ a tank, or _____ listening _____ the sounds _____ birds. These (10) (11) (12) (13)
activities are very calming.

8 CHAPTER

A Healthy Diet for Everyone

Prereading Preparation

1. Look at the photographs. Describe the two meals. Which meal do you think is healthier? Why?

2. Work with one or two partners. Fill in the chart on page 151. What food do you think is healthy? What food is not?

3. Why is it important to have a healthy diet?

Food That Is Healthy	Food That Is Not Healthy

4 Read the title of this passage. People in different cultures and countries eat different kinds of food. What health food suggestions can you make that everyone around the world can follow? What does "A Healthy Diet for Everyone" mean?

Track 15

A Healthy Diet for Everyone

1 Everyone knows that we must eat food in order to live. However, sometimes,
2 people are confused about what type of food is healthy, and what kind of food
3 can be harmful to our health. The USDA[1] has prepared a food guide to help
4 people learn about which types of food are the healthiest to eat. The food guide
5 describes six basic food groups: meat (beef, fish, chicken, etc.), dairy (milk,
6 yogurt, cheese, etc.), grains (bread, cereal, rice, etc.), fruit, and vegetables. The
7 last group is fats, oil, and sweets. The USDA also suggests how much of each
8 food group is healthy to eat daily. Although this guide was prepared by the
9 U.S. government, it is very useful for people all over the world.

[1]The United States Department of Agriculture. The USDA's responsibility is to control the quality of food in the United States.

10	As a result of years of research, we know that too much animal fat is bad for
11	our health. For example, Americans eat a lot of meat and only a small amount of
12	grains, fruit, and vegetables. Because of their diet, they have a high rate of cancer
13	and heart disease. In Japan, in contrast, people eat large amounts of grains and
14	very little meat. The Japanese also have a very low rate of cancer and heart
15	disease. In fact, the Japanese live longer than almost anyone else in the world.
16	Unfortunately, when Japanese people move to the United States, the rate of heart
17	disease and cancer increases as their diet changes. Moreover, as hamburgers,
18	ice cream, and other high-fat foods become popular in Japan, the rate of heart
19	disease and cancer is increasing there as well. People are also eating more meat
20	and dairy products in other countries, such as Cuba, Mauritius, and Hungary.
21	Not surprisingly, the disease rate in these countries is increasing along with the
22	change in diet. Consequently, doctors everywhere advise people to eat more
23	grains, fruit, and vegetables, and eat less meat and fewer dairy products.
24	A healthy diet is important for children as well as adults. When adults have
25	poor eating habits, their children usually do, too. After all, children eat the same
26	way as their parents. When parents eat healthy food, the children will learn to
27	enjoy it, too. Then they will develop good eating habits. Doctors advise parents
28	to give their children healthier snacks such as fruit, vegetables, and juice.
29	Everyone wants to live a long, healthy life. We know that the food we eat affects
30	us in different ways. For instance, doctors believe that fruit and vegetables can
31	actually prevent many different diseases. On the other hand, animal fat can cause
32	disease. We can improve our diet now and enjoy many years of healthy living.

A Fact-Finding Exercise

Read the passage once. Then read the following statements. Check whether they are True or False. If a statement is false, rewrite the statement so that it is true. Then go back to the passage and find the line that supports your answer.

1 _____ True _____ False   There are six basic food groups.

_____

2 _____ True _____ False   People can choose food from each group every day.

_____

3 _____ True _____ False   Most Americans eat a lot of meat.

_____

4 _____ True _____ False   Most Japanese eat very few grains.

_____

5 _____ True _____ False   There is a high rate of cancer and heart disease in Japan.

_____

6 _____ True _____ False   Doctors think it is a good idea for people to eat less meat.

_____

7 _____ True _____ False   It is not important for children to have a healthy diet.

_____

8 _____ True _____ False   Children usually eat differently than their parents.

_____

9 _____ True _____ False   Doctors believe that fruit and vegetables cause different diseases.

_____

B Skimming and Scanning Exercise

PART 1

Skim through the passage. Then read the following statements. Choose the one that is the correct main idea of the reading.

    a. The kind of diet we have can cause or prevent diseases.
    b. Doctors advise people to eat more fruit, vegetables, and grains.
    c. Eating meat causes cancer and heart disease.

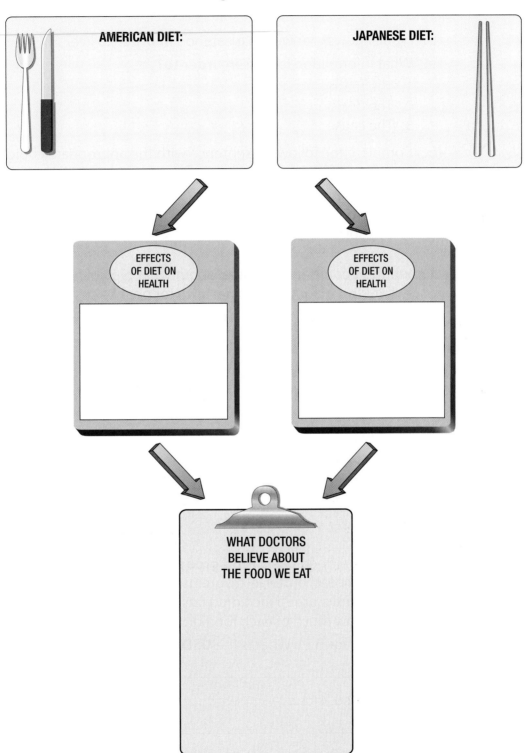

PART 2

Scan the passage. Work with a partner to fill in the flowchart below with information from the reading.

AMERICAN DIET:

JAPANESE DIET:

EFFECTS OF DIET ON HEALTH

EFFECTS OF DIET ON HEALTH

WHAT DOCTORS BELIEVE ABOUT THE FOOD WE EAT

Reading Analysis

Read each question carefully. Either circle the letter or the number of the correct answer or write your answer in the blank space.

1 Everyone knows that we must eat food **in order to** live.

   a. What information follows **in order to?**

      1. The reason
      2. The decision
      3. The cause

   b. Complete the following sentence with the appropriate choice. Cindy went to the supermarket in order to

      1. walk to the store
      2. learn how to cook
      3. buy some food

2 Sometimes people are **confused** about what type of food is healthy, and what **kind** of food can be **harmful** for our health.

   a. In these sentences, which word is a synonym for **kind?**

   _____

   b. What does **confused** mean?

      1. Mixed up
      2. Clear
      3. Unhappy

   c. What does **harmful** mean?

      1. Bad
      2. Good
      3. Easy

3 The **USDA** described **basic food groups:** meat (beef, fish, chicken, etc.), dairy (milk, cheese, butter, etc.), grains (bread, cereals, rice, etc.), fruit, vegetables, and a group including fats, oils, and sweets. The USDA suggested how much of each food group was healthy to eat **daily.**

   a. Refer to page 151. What is the **USDA?**

   _____

   b. How do you know?

   _____

c. The information at the bottom of page 151 is called a

_____

d. What are the basic food groups? Give examples of each group.

1. _____

2. _____

3. _____

4. _____

5. _____

6. _____

e. What does **daily** mean?

1. Every day
2. A lot of
3. A little of

4 Americans eat a lot of meat and only a small amount of grains, fruit, and vegetables. In Japan, **in contrast,** people eat large amounts of grains and very little meat. The Japanese also have a very low rate of cancer and heart disease. **In fact,** the Japanese live longer than **anyone else** in the world.

a. What information follows **in contrast?**

1. A similar idea
2. An opposite idea
3. The same idea

b. What information follows **in fact?**

1. More information about the same idea
2. Contrasting information about the same idea
3. Surprising information about the same idea

c. What does **anyone else** mean?

1. All other people
2. Some other people
3. Most other people

5 **Unfortunately,** when Japanese people move to the United States, the rate of heart disease and cancer increases **as** their diet changes. **Moreover,** as hamburgers, ice cream, and other high-fat foods become popular in Japan, the rate of heart disease and cancer increases **there,** too.

a. What follows **unfortunately?**

1. Something lucky
2. Something bad
3. Something false

b. What does **as** mean?

1. When
2. So
3. And

c. What does **moreover** mean?

1. However
2. Also
3. Then

d. What are some examples of high-fat foods?

_____

e. Where does **there** refer to?

1. In the United States
2. In Cuba
3. In Japan

6 People are also eating more meat and dairy products in other countries **such as** Cuba, Mauritius, and Hungary. **Not surprisingly,** the disease rate in these countries is increasing along with the change in diet. **Consequently,** doctors everywhere advise people to eat more grains, fruit, and vegetables, and less meat and fewer dairy products.

a. What does **such as** mean?

1. For example
2. Instead of
3. Except in

b. What information follows **not surprisingly?**

1. Information that is hard to believe
2. Information that is not true
3. Information that is easy to believe

c. What does **consequently** mean?

1. In addition
2. As a result
3. In fact

7 A healthy diet is important for children **as well as** adults.

   a. This sentence means that a healthy diet

      1. is more important for children than it is for adults
      2. is more important for adults than it is for children
      3. is equally important for both adults and children

   b. **As well as** means

      1. and also
      2. but not
      3. instead of

8 When adults have poor eating habits, their children usually do, too. **After all,** children eat the same way as their parents.

   a. The first sentence means

      1. the children usually have better eating habits
      2. the children also have poor eating habits

   b. Read the second sentence again. Then read the following sentence and complete it with the appropriate choice. José speaks Spanish fluently. After all,

      1. he lived in Venezuela for 15 years
      2. he reads many books about South America

9 Most doctors agree that fruit and vegetables can actually **prevent** many different diseases. **On the other hand,** animal fat can **cause** disease.

   a. What is the connection between **prevent** and **cause?**

      1. They have similar meanings.
      2. They have opposite meanings.

   b. What does **prevent** mean?

      1. To keep from happening
      2. To make happen

   c. What information follows **on the other hand?**

      1. A similar idea
      2. An example of the idea
      3. An opposite idea

   d. Read the following sentences. Complete the second sentence with the appropriate choice. I may visit many different places on my vacation. On the other hand,

      1. I may go to museums, zoos, parks, and beaches
      2. I may stay at home and relax

D Dictionary Skills

Read the dictionary entry for each word and think about the context of the sentence. Write the number of the appropriate definition on the line next to the word. Then choose the sentence with the correct answer.

1 | **confuse** *v.* [T] -fused, -fusing, -fuses **1** to mix things up: *He sent the wrong reports because he confused them with other ones.* **2** to mix up mentally so that one cannot understand or think clearly: *The teacher's question confused him.*

Sometimes, people are **confused** about what type of food is healthy, and what kind of food can be bad for our health.

a. **confused:** _____
b. 1. Sometimes, people mix up healthy food and unhealthy food.
   2. Sometimes, people feel mixed up and cannot understand which kinds of food are healthy and which kinds are not.

2 | **prevent** *v.* [T] **1** to stop from happening: *He prevented an accident by braking his car just in time.* **2** to stop s.o. from doing s.t.: *The rain prevented me from going.*

Doctors believe that fruit and vegetables can actually **prevent** many different diseases.

a. **prevent:** _____
b. 1. Doctors believe that fruit and vegetables can help people avoid many different diseases.
   2. Doctors believe that fruit and vegetables can stop diseases from making people sick.

3 | **suggest** *v.* [T] **1** to propose s.t. to do or to offer an idea for consideration: *He suggested that we have lunch at the hotel.* **2** to bring (an idea) to mind, to indicate: *This picture suggests an ancient battle scene.* | | *The results of the test suggested that I was ill.*

The USDA **suggested** how much of each food group was healthy to eat daily.

a. **suggest:** _____
b. 1. The USDA brought to mind how much of each food group was healthy to eat daily.
   2. The USDA offered people an idea of how much of each food group was healthy to eat daily.

Word Forms

In English, some verbs become nouns by adding the suffix -ment, for example, announce (v.), announcement (n.). Complete each sentence with the correct form of the words on the left. **Write all the verbs in the simple present tense. They may be affirmative or negative. The nouns may be singular or plural.**

improve (v.)

improvement (n.)

1 Manufacturers have made many _____ in computers in the last ten years. For example, they are smaller, faster, and more dependable. Manufacturers _____ their products to satisfy their customers.

agree (v.)

agreement (n.)

2 Some people are vegetarians. They think that eating meat is unhealthy. However, Faye _____ with the vegetarians. Faye believes that eating meat occasionally causes no health problems. However, she is in _____ with the idea that fruit and vegetables are very healthy.

encourage (v.)

encouragement (n.)

3 Jason is my best friend. He always _____ me when I have a difficult problem. In fact, his _____ has often helped me to succeed.

develop (v.)

development (n.)

4 Scientists are working to _____ a cure for all kinds of cancer. The _____ of a cure will be welcome all around the world.

enjoy (v.)

enjoyment (n.)

5 I _____ going to the movies alone. I prefer to go with a friend. Watching a movie with a friend adds to my _____.

In English, the noun form and the verb form of some words are the same, for example, *move (v.), move (n.)*. Complete each sentence with the correct form of the word on the left. Circle *(v.)* if you are using a verb, or *(n.)* if you are using a noun. **Write all the verbs in the simple present tense. They may be affirmative or negative. The nouns may be singular or plural.**

research   ① Dr. Johnson _____ cures for cancer. She does all
                    (v., n.)

her _____ on heart disease.
    (v., n.)

increase   ② During the summer, the temperature _____ to
                    (v., n.)

about 30°. This significant _____ in temperature
                            (v., n.)

usually makes many people uncomfortable.

taste   ③ I like the sweet _____ of fruit, such as cherries,
                    (v., n.)

pears, and peaches. Lemons _____ sweet, however.
                            (v., n.)

They are very sour.

change   ④ In some areas of the world, there are four _____ in
                    (v., n.)

seasons: spring, summer, fall, and winter. However, in other

countries, the climate _____ at all. It is the same all
                        (v., n.)

year. There is only one season.

cause

5 There are many _____ of cancer. For example,
(v., n.)

sometimes, exposure to the sun _____ skin cancer.
(v., n.)

Word Partnership	Use *cause* with:
v.	**determine the** cause, **support a** cause
n.	cause **of death,** cause **an accident,** cause **cancer,** cause **problems,** cause **a reaction,** cause **for concern**

F

Vocabulary in Context

confuse *(v.)*	in order to	suggest *(v.)*
in contrast	not surprisingly *(adv.)*	unfortunately *(adv.)*
in fact	prevent *(v.)*	

Read the following sentences. Complete each blank space with the correct word or phrase from the list above. Use each word or phrase only once.

1 Leon eats fresh fruit and vegetables daily. His brother Sam eats cake and

cookies every day. _____, Leon is healthier than Sam.

2 Viola wanted to go swimming at the beach yesterday. _____,

it rained all day, so she stayed home.

3 Michael and his brother, Tom, look very different. Michael is short and has

light hair. _____, Tom is tall and has dark hair.

4 When Harry and Bill do dangerous work, they _____ injury by being especially careful.

5 Jane loves to read books. _____, she reads about 100 books a year.

6 If you want to get up at 4:00 A.M. to go fishing, I _____ that you go to bed before 8:00 P.M.

7 _____ lose weight, you need to exercise more and eat less.

8 Leigh's directions always _____ me. When she gives me directions, I usually get lost.

G

Think About It

Read the following questions and think about the answers. Write your answer below each question. Then compare your answers with those of your classmates.

1 Why did the USDA prepare a food guide for Americans?

_____

_____

_____

2 Why are fats, oils, and sweets grouped together?

_____

_____

_____

3 Why do Japanese people change their diet when they move to the United States?

_____

_____

_____

H Another Look

Read the following passage about reasons why people eat when they're not hungry. Then answer the questions that follow.

Why Do I Eat When I'm Not Hungry?

1   The next time you want to eat something, ask yourself a question. Are you
2   _really_ hungry? If you answer "No," then ask yourself why you want to eat when
3   your body is not really hungry. The following reasons may help you understand
4   why you do so.

5   • I'M BORED. Sometimes we are bored and don't have anything better to do.
6   When this happens, and you start to walk into the kitchen, stop yourself.
7   Go to another part of the house, or go for a walk.
8   • IT TASTES GOOD. Sometimes it does, but sometimes we eat anything we
9   can find in the kitchen, even if it really isn't that great tasting. When I'm
10   dieting, I like to eat food that I _really_ enjoy. Eat less of it, and enjoy it.
11 • I HAVE A LOT OF STRESS. This is often a common reason for eating. I often
12   eat because of stress, not because I am hungry. I try to read a book,
13   or exercise instead.
14 • TV MAKES ME WANT TO EAT. I rarely watched TV when I was thin. Then
15   I started to watch TV almost every evening, and I gained 45 pounds. Evening
16   TV programs have many food commercials that make me run to the kitchen
17   for a snack. My best advice is to stop watching evening television.

18 • BECAUSE I'M REALLY THIRSTY. Sometimes people eat because they are
19   thirsty. Instead of having something to drink, people eat something that is
20   often fattening. The next time you feel hungry, drink some water.

21 If your stomach is making noise, it is time to eat. If you want food between
22 meals when your stomach is *not* making noise, don't eat. Remember, you
23 should give your body some kind of nutrition three times a day. If you do have
24 to eat between meals, eat a piece of fruit or a vegetable. Try to think about
25 what and why you are eating the next time you want a snack. Ask yourself,
26 "Why am I eating?"

Questions for Another Look

1 What is the main idea of the story?
   a. There are many reasons why people eat when they are hungry.
   b. There are many reasons why people eat when they are not hungry.
   c. Watching television makes people eat when they are not hungry.

UNIT 4   HEALTHY LIVING

2 What are some reasons why people eat when they are not hungry?

a. _____

b. _____

c. _____

d. _____

e. _____

3 Instead of eating when you are not hungry, what are some other things you can do?

_____

_____

_____

_____

Topics for Discussion and Writing

1 Is there a high rate of heart disease or cancer in your country? What do you think are some reasons for this?

2 The reading passage discusses a healthy diet as a way to prevent disease. Work with a classmate. Make a list of other ways to prevent disease. Compare your list with those of your classmates.

3 Do you have children? What kind of food do you give them? Why? Do they enjoy the food? If you don't have children, imagine that you do. What kind of food do you give them? Why?

4 **Write in your journal.** Describe the ways you help yourself live a healthy life.

Follow-Up Activities

1 The U.S. Department of Health and Human Services has prepared a Food Guide Pyramid to help people build a healthy diet for themselves. Read the suggested daily servings of each food group. Read the definitions of a serving for each food group.

a. Use the Food Guide Pyramid and the serving descriptions to plan a one-day healthy diet. Write your diet in the chart on page 169. Then show your servings in the pyramid on page 170.

b. Compare your one-day healthy diet with those of your classmates. In what ways are they similar? In what ways are they different?

What's a serving?

milk, yogurt, cheese, ice cream, frozen yogurt
(2–4 servings daily) Most choices should be fat-free or low-fat.
- 1 cup of milk
- 1 cup of yogurt
- 1 ½ ounces of cheese

vegetable group (3–5 servings daily) They can be raw or cooked, and fresh, frozen, canned, or dried. 100% vegetable juice counts as a member of the vegetable group.
- 6 oz. juice
- ½ cup cut-up vegetable
- 1 cup leafy green vegetable

fruit group (2–3 servings daily) They can be fresh, canned, frozen, or dried. Whole fruit is a better choice than fruit juice.
- 1 medium apple, banana, orange, etc.
- 1 melon wedge
- ½ cup chopped fruit or berries
- ¼ cup dried fruit

meat and beans group (meat, poultry, fish, dry beans, eggs, and nuts) (2–6 servings daily)
- 2–3 ounces cooked meat, fish, or poultry
- dry beans: ½ cup cooked dried peas or beans
- 1 egg
- 2 tablespoons seeds or nuts

grains group (6–11 servings daily) Make at least half your grains whole grains.
- 1 slice of bread, preferably whole grain bread
- 1 ounce of prepared (dry) cereal
- ½ cup cooked cereal, such as oatmeal
- ½ cup cooked rice, preferably brown rice
- ½ cup cooked pasta
- Popcorn is healthy, too!

A One-Day Healthy Diet					
Breakfast	(Snack)	Lunch	(Snack)	Dinner	(Snack)

MyPyramid.gov
STEPS TO A HEALTHIER YOU

2 Larry is a student at the state university. The following menu shows what he usually eats for breakfast, lunch, and dinner. What changes can you make to Larry's menu in order to make it healthier for him?

Breakfast:
two eggs
two slices of white bread with butter
one cup of coffee with cream and sugar

Lunch:
one large chocolate ice-cream cone

Dinner:
one cheeseburger on a roll
one large order of French fries
an order of broccoli
lettuce and tomatoes

Late-night snack:
a bag of potato chips
an apple

3 Alone or with one or more classmates, go to a fast-food restaurant. Order a *healthy* meal. Report back to the class. Describe the meal you ate and explain why it was nutritious.

4 Alone or with a student from your country, prepare a menu for a typical breakfast, lunch, and dinner in your country. Then talk to a student from another country and show the student your menu. Explain why you think your diet is healthy. Then ask the other student to explain why he or she thinks his/her diet is healthy. Compare your menu with the student's menu from a different country. Discuss which diet you both think is healthier.

K Word Search

Read the words listed below. Find them in the puzzle and circle them. They may be written in any direction.

avoid	cholesterol	fruit	prevent
cancer	diet	healthy	recommend
children	fattening	parents	vegetables

O	C	V	Y	D	N	E	M	M	O	C	E	R	B	T
Y	T	H	R	Z	F	V	C	Y	H	T	L	A	E	H
C	H	I	L	D	R	E	N	O	N	Z	H	I	B	W
J	T	V	N	J	U	G	L	L	A	S	D	C	N	Y
P	V	F	A	T	T	E	N	I	N	G	Q	D	F	W
P	A	C	G	W	S	T	D	X	F	P	Z	E	W	M
X	L	R	A	T	H	A	I	X	R	C	Y	B	A	F
P	E	Y	E	N	P	B	O	E	U	K	E	Z	C	R
J	L	R	Q	N	C	L	V	O	I	G	M	R	E	Q
R	O	I	K	P	T	E	A	D	T	U	G	S	Z	G
L	C	N	I	D	N	S	R	P	Q	Z	X	M	V	M
Q	Z	V	K	T	G	T	X	E	T	V	M	W	J	S

Crossword Puzzle

Read the clues on the next page. Write the answers in the correct spaces in the puzzle.

Crossword Puzzle Clues

ACROSS CLUES

  4. Study very carefully

  5. As a result

  7. The opposite of **yes**

  9. The opposite of **on**

11. Also; furthermore

12. In good physical condition

13. Rice and cereals are _____.

14. Keep from happening

17. The opposite of **down**

19. When we make many _____, we make things better.

20. The opposite of **no**

22. Illness; sickness

23. The opposite of **bottom**

DOWN CLUES

  1. I am. She _____.

  2. Every day

  3. Type

  5. _____ is a very serious illness.

  6. Unhappily

  8. You have a choice: you can have either coffee _____ tea.

10. _____ and vegetables are very healthy for us to eat.

13. There are six basic food _____.

15. Milk, butter, and ice cream are _____ products.

16. I am _____. I don't understand what you said.

18. He is. We _____.

21. Chicken, pork, and beef are types of _____.

22. Everything we eat is part of our _____.

Grammar Cloze Quiz

Read the passage. Complete each blank space with one of the words or phrases listed below. You may use them more than once. In addition, *there may be more than one correct answer.*

a high rate of	fewer	more
a lot of	large amounts of	too much
a small amount of	less	very little
a very low rate of		

As a result of years of research, we know that _____ (1) animal fat is bad for our health. For example, Americans eat _____ (2) meat, and _____ (3) grains, fruit, and vegetables. Because of their diet, they have _____ (4) cancer and heart disease. In Japan, in contrast, people eat _____ (5) grains and _____ (6) meat. The Japanese also have _____ (7) cancer and heart disease. In fact, the Japanese live longer than anyone else in the world. Consequently, doctors everywhere advise people to eat _____ (8) grains, fruit, and vegetables, and eat _____ (9) meat and _____ (10) dairy products.

UNIT 4 | DISCUSSION

1. There are many steps that we can take to help ourselves have a healthy life. With a classmate or in a small group, discuss what you can do to have a healthy life.

2. With a classmate or in a small group, discuss how you will change the way you eat every day to have a healthier diet.

International Scientists

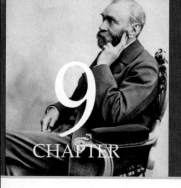

9
CHAPTER

Alfred Nobel:
A Man of Peace

Prereading Preparation

1. Look at the photograph below. This medal is a Nobel Prize. Alfred Nobel's image is in the center of the medal. What are the reasons why Alfred Nobel is famous?

   a. He established the Nobel Prize.
   b. He lived in the nineteenth century.
   c. He invented dynamite.
   d. He was Swedish.

2. What do you know about Alfred Nobel? Work with a partner. Make a list.

   _____

   _____

   _____

3 Read the title of this passage. Why do you think Alfred Nobel is called a man of peace?

_____

_____

Alfred Nobel: A Man of Peace

Track 17

1　　The headline in the newspaper announced the death of Alfred Nobel on
2　April 13, 1888. The reporter called him a salesman of death, "The Dynamite
3　King," because he invented this powerful explosive. In fact, Alfred Nobel's
4　dynamite business had made him a very rich man. The newspaper story
5　continued, giving Alfred Nobel's age, nationality, and other information about
6　his business. However, the words "The Dynamite King" were all that the
7　55-year-old Swedish man read.
8　　Alfred Nobel sadly put down the newspaper. No, he wasn't dead—his
9　brother Ludwig had died the day before, and the French newspaper had
10　made a mistake. All the same, Alfred Nobel was disturbed. Was this the way
11　the world was going to remember him? He did not like that idea at all. He
12　had spent his life working for peace in the world. He hated violence and war.
13　He had invented dynamite to _save_ lives—lives that were lost because other
14　explosives were dangerous to use. He wanted people to remember him as a
15　man of peace.
16　　Alfred Nobel invented dynamite at a perfect moment in time. Many
17　countries were beginning to build railroads and tunnels, and needed a safe,
18　powerful explosive to construct railroad tracks through mountains. People also
19　needed dynamite to blow up stone in order to construct buildings, dams, and
20　roads. Alfred Nobel invented dynamite for these peaceful uses. Moreover, he
21　believed that if all countries had the same powerful weapons, they would see
22　how impossible war was, and wars would end. In fact, this was a popular idea
23　of his day.
24　　Nobel was very upset about the image that the world had of him, but he
25　did not know what to do about it. He thought about his problem for years.
26　He wanted to think of the best way for people to use his fortune of $9 million
27　after his death. Then in 1895, an adventurer named Salomon August Andree
28　made plans for an expedition to reach the North Pole. People all over the

29 world were excited about Andree's journey. Nobel read about Andree's plan,
30 too, and had an inspiration. He finally knew what to do with his fortune. He
31 wrote his Last Will and Testament[1]. In his will, he instructed people to use all
32 of his money for an annual award as an honor to leaders of science, literature,
33 and world peace. He stated that these leaders could be men or women of any
34 nationality.
35   Alfred Nobel died on December 10, 1896, at the age of 63. He was unmarried
36 and had no children. People all over the world wondered who was going to get
37 Nobel's money. They were amazed when they learned of Alfred Nobel's plan to
38 award annual prizes in the fields of physics, chemistry, medicine, literature, and
39 peace. The first Nobel Prizes were awarded in 1901, and they very soon became
40 the greatest honor that a person could receive in these fields. In 1969, an award
41 for economics was added.
42   The report of Alfred Nobel's death had been a mistake, but the decision that
43 he made because of this error gave the world the image he wanted. Alfred Nobel
44 established the Nobel Prize, and the world thinks of him the way he wanted to
45 be remembered: Alfred Nobel, man of peace.

[1]Last Will and Testament: A legal paper that states how a person wishes his or her possessions to be distributed after his or her death.

Fact-Finding Exercise

Read the passage once. Then read the following statements. Check whether they are True or False. If a statement is false, rewrite it so that it is true. Then go back to the passage and find the line that supports your answer.

1 _____ True ___✓___ False   Alfred Nobel wanted people to remember him as "The Dynamite King."

_____

2 _____ True ___✓___ False   Alfred Nobel died in 1888.

_____

3 __✓__ True _____ False   Alfred Nobel invented dynamite.

_____

4 __✓__ True _____ False   Alfred Nobel hated violence.

_____

5 _____ True ___✓___ False   Only men can receive a Nobel Prize.

_____

6 _____ True ___✓___ False   In 1895, Salomon August Andree received the first Nobel Prize.

_____

Skimming and Scanning Exercise

PART 1

Skim through the passage. Then read the following statements. Choose the one that is the correct main idea of the reading.

    a. Alfred Nobel wrote his will after Andree went to the North Pole.
    b. The Nobel Prize is an internationally famous award.
    c. Alfred Nobel was a peaceful man who gave the world a great prize.

Scan the passage. Work with a partner to fill in the chart with information from the reading.

ALFRED NOBEL		
Accomplishment	Reason	Result
He invented dynamite.		
He established the Nobel Prize.		

Reading Analysis

Read each question carefully. Either circle the letter or the number of the correct answer or write your answer in the space provided.

1 The newspaper story gave Alfred Nobel's age, nationality, and other information about his business. **However,** the words "The Dynamite King" were **all** that the 55-year-old Swedish man read.

a. What does **however** mean?

1. And
2. But
3. Then

b. Complete the following sentence with the appropriate choice. Robert wanted to go to the beach. However,

1. it rained, so he stayed home
2. he asked his friends to go with him
3. he brought his lunch and a big umbrella

c. "The words 'The Dynamite King' were **all** that the 55-year-old Swedish man read." What does this mean?

    1. He read everything.
    ②. These three words were the only words he read.
    3. He read these words completely.

2 The French newspaper made a mistake about Nobel. Ludwig Nobel died, not Alfred Nobel. **All the same,** Alfred Nobel was disturbed. What do these sentences mean?

    a. Because the news was a mistake, Alfred was not upset anymore.
    b. It did not matter that the news was a mistake. Alfred was still upset.

3 The world was going to remember him as "The Dynamite King." Alfred Nobel did not like that idea **at all.** This sentence means that

    a. he liked the idea a little
    b. he liked the idea a lot
    c. he did not like anything about the idea

4 Nobel invented dynamite to save lives—lives that were lost because other explosives were dangerous to use. What follows the dash (**—**)?

    a. A contrast
    b. An example
    c. An explanation

5 Alfred Nobel invented dynamite for peaceful uses. **Moreover,** he believed that if all countries had the same powerful weapons, they would see how impossible war was, and wars would end. This was a popular idea of **his day.**

    a. **Moreover** means

        1. however
        2. in addition
        3. as a result

    b. Complete the following sentence with the correct choice.

        Robert needed to learn English because he wanted to go to college in the United States. Moreover,

        1. he had to speak English to get a good job
        2. he hated to study and was a poor student

    c. **His day** refers to

        1. the day Nobel invented dynamite
        2. the year 1895
        3. the time that he lived

6 Nobel wanted to think of the best way for people to use his **fortune** of $9 million after his death.

What is a synonym of **fortune?**

   a. Idea
   b. Plan
   c. Wealth

7 In 1895, Alfred Nobel wrote his **Last Will and Testament.** In his will, he instructed people to use all of his money for an annual award.

   a. Look at page 178. What is a **Last Will and Testament?**

   _____

   _____

   b. How do you know?

   _____

   _____

   c. This information is called a

   _____

8 Alfred Nobel had a plan to award annual prizes in the **fields** of physics, chemistry, medicine, literature, and peace.

   a. What does **fields** mean?

      1. Occupation; job
      2. Subject; area
      3. Outdoor area

   b. Give some examples of **fields.**

   _____

9 The report of Alfred Nobel's death was a **mistake**, but the decision that he made because of this error gave the world the image he wanted.

In this sentence, which word is a synonym of **mistake?**

   _____

D

Dictionary Skills

Read the dictionary entry for each word and think about the context of the sentence. Write the number of the appropriate definition on the line next to the word. In addition, circle *noun, verb,* or *adjective* where indicated. Then choose the sentence with the correct answer.

1

> **perfect** *adj.* **1** the best possible: *a perfect score* (or) *record* || *If only the world were perfect!* **2** complete and faultless, with nothing wrong or missing: *This car is in perfect condition.* **3** appropriate and satisfactory in every respect: *The holiday decorations were perfect.* **4** total, complete, thorough: *a perfect fool* || *a perfect stranger*
>
> —*v.* [T] to make perfect, flawless, excellent: *She perfected her style of playing the piano by practicing eight hours a day.*
>
> —*n.* (in grammar) a verb tense that shows action completed at a certain time: *In the sentence, "I had finished my dinner when she phoned," the verb "had finished" is in the past perfect.*

Alfred Nobel invented dynamite at a **perfect** moment in time. Many countries were beginning to build railroads and tunnels and needed a safe, powerful explosive to construct railroad tracks through mountains.

   a. **perfect:** _____ (adjective / verb / noun)

   b. 1. Nobel invented dynamite at a satisfactory moment in time.

       2. Nobel invented dynamite at a complete and faultless moment in time.

       3. Nobel invented dynamite at the best possible moment in time.

2

> **disturb** *v.* [T] **1** to interrupt: *Bad dreams disturbed her sleep.* **2** to worry, upset: *The bad news disturbed him.*

The newspaper article that described Alfred Nobel as "The Dynamite King" **disturbed** him. Nobel did not want the world to remember him that way. He hated violence and war.

   a. **disturb:** _____ (adjective / verb / noun)

   b. 1. The newspaper article that described Alfred Nobel as "The Dynamite King" upset him.

       2. The newspaper article that described Alfred Nobel as "The Dynamite King" interrupted him.

3 **award** *v.* [T] **1** to give a prize (honor, praise, etc.) to s.o.: *The school principal awarded a prize in history to the best student.* **2** to give, grant: *A buyer awarded a contract to the supplier.*

—*n.* a prize (honor, praise, etc.) given to s.o. for outstanding performance: *The teacher gave her best student an award.*

In his will, Alfred Nobel instructed people to use all of his money for an annual **award** to honor leaders of science, literature, and world peace.

   a. **award:** _____ (adjective / verb / noun)

   b. 1. Alfred Nobel instructed people to use all of his money for an annual grant to honor leaders of science, literature, and world peace.

      2. Alfred Nobel instructed people to use all of his money for an annual prize to honor leaders of science, literature, and world peace.

4 **honor** *n.* **1** [U] one's good reputation (for honesty, integrity, etc.): *He is a man of honor and is totally trustworthy.* **2** [U] (for a woman) virtue, morality: *Her honor is above question.* **3** [C; U] praise, recognition from others: *She has the honor of being given an award.* **4** *sing.* privilege, distinction: *The mayor has the honor of introducing the President to the audience.* **5** [U] a term of address for a mayor or a judge: *His Honor the Mayor attended the meeting.* **6** **on one's honor:** an agreement to do s.t. based on one's word, integrity: *You may take the examination without supervision, and you are on your honor not to cheat.* **7** **with honors:** with high academic marks: *He graduated with honors.*

—*v.* [T] **1** to praise, give recognition to: *She was honored by the mayor with a good citizenship award.* **2** to show respect: *The son honors his parents by caring for them.* **3** to fulfill a promise or obligation: *She honored her student loans by paying them.*

أنسترمى

In his will, Alfred Nobel instructed people to use all of his money for an annual award to **honor** leaders of science, literature, and world peace.

   a. **honor:** _____ (adjective / verb / noun)

   b. 1. In his will, Alfred Nobel instructed people to use all of his money for an annual award to fulfill his obligation to leaders of science, literature, and world peace.

      2. In his will, Alfred Nobel instructed people to use all of his money for an annual award to give recognition to leaders of science, literature, and world peace.

      3. In his will, Alfred Nobel instructed people to use all of his money for an annual award to show respect to leaders of science, literature, and world peace.

E Word Forms

In English, some verbs become nouns by adding the suffix *-ion* or *-ation,* for example, *suggest (v.), suggestion (n.).* Be careful of spelling changes, for example, *combine (v.), combination (n.).* Complete each sentence with the correct form of the words on the left. **Write all the verbs in the simple past tense. They may be affirmative or negative. The nouns may be singular or plural.**

instruct *(v.)*

instruction *(n.)*

1. The teacher *instruct* _____ the students to write their compositions in pen, to skip a line, and to put their names on their papers. The students followed her *instruction* carefully.

invent *(v.)*

invention *(n.)*

2. Thomas Edison, an American, *invented* more than 1,000 useful items. His *invention* include the light bulb, sound movies, and the phonograph, or record player.

construct *(v.)*

construction *(n.)*

3. The company finished the *construct* of their new office building. The company *constructed* the building of steel. They built it with bricks and wood instead.

inspire *(v.)*

inspiration *(n.)*

4. When the general gave a speech to his soldiers, he _____ them to action. As a result of the general's _____, the soldiers won the difficult battle.

continue *(v.)*

continuation *(n.)*

5. When Jenny graduated from high school, she _____ her education immediately. She went to college several years later. The _____ of her education had to wait until she saved enough money.

In English, there are several ways that verbs change to nouns. Some verbs become nouns by adding the suffix *-ment,* for example, *improve (v.), improvement (n.).* Complete each sentence with the correct form of the words on the left. **Write all the verbs in the simple past tense. They may be affirmative or negative. The nouns may be singular or plural.**

announce *(v.)*

announcement *(n.)*

1 Carol and Simon _____ their engagement yesterday. They plan to get married in two months. Their happy _____ surprised their friends.

excite *(v.)*

excitement *(n.)*

2 Lloyd went to a baseball game yesterday, but the game _____ him at all. He prefers to watch soccer games. However, I enjoy watching baseball games. I think there is a lot of _____ in a baseball game.

amaze *(v.)*

amazement *(n.)*

3 The magician was very talented, and he _____ the children with his wonderful tricks. He smiled at their look of _____ when he pulled a rabbit from his hat.

state *(v.)*

statement *(n.)*

4 The Governor made a few _____ last night. In his speech, he _____ that he planned to run for reelection next year and that he also planned to cut taxes.

establish *(v.)*

establishment *(n.)*

5 The Board of Directors discussed the formal _____ of a law school at the university ten years ago. However, they _____ the law school until this year.

Word Partnership	Use *establish* with:
n.	establish **control**, establish **independence**, establish **rules**, establish **contact**, establish **relations**, establish *someone's* **identity**

F Vocabulary in Context

all the same	disturb *(v.)*	fortune *(n.)*	however *(conj.)*
amaze *(v.)*	field *(n.)*	honor *(n.)*	mistake *(n.)*

Read the following sentences. Complete each blank space with the correct word or phrase from the list above. Use each word or phrase only once.

1. Ji Soo is going into the _____ of medicine. She wants to become a doctor.

2. David wants to take a vacation to Hawaii. _____, he doesn't have enough money now, so he's going to wait until next year.

3. The art in Sophia's home is worth a _____. Her family owns several paintings by very famous artists. Each painting is worth over a million dollars.

4. Magicians always _____ people with their tricks. They can make a rabbit disappear, or cut a woman in half.

5. I made a _____ in my paper. I wrote "he do" instead of "he does."

6. Never _____ Susan when she is studying. She needs to concentrate on her books.

7. We were cold and tired from our long walk in the country. _____, when we came home, we decided to go to the movies after dinner.

8. The University surprised a graduating student with a special _____ for her volunteer work with young children during her summer vacations.

Think About It

Read the following questions and think about the answers. Write your answers below each question. Then, compare your answers with those of your classmates.

1 Alfred Nobel invented dynamite to help people build railroads, tunnels, buildings, and dams, but the reporter in the story called Nobel "a salesman of death." Why?

_____

_____

_____

_____

_____

2 How did Nobel earn his fortune of $9 million?

_____

_____

_____

_____

_____

3 Nobel established the Nobel Prize so that people would remember him as a man of peace. Can you think of another reason why he wanted to give prizes to people who were leaders in their fields?

_____

_____

_____

_____

_____

Another Look

Read the following description of how Nobel Prize winners are chosen. Then answer the questions that follow.

Track 18

Choosing Nobel Prize Winners

1   Alfred Nobel gave more than $9 million of his fortune to establish annual
2 Nobel Prizes. According to Nobel's instructions, the money is given to people
3 who help humankind in some outstanding way in five fields: physics, chemistry,
4 physiology (or medicine), literature, and peace. In addition to the cash prize,
5 each Nobel Prize winner receives a gold medal.
6   The Nobel Foundation is the legal owner of the prize funds, but it does not
7 award the prizes. The Foundation follows a list of Alfred Nobel's rules. One of
8 the rules states that not all the prizes must be given out each year. In fact, no
9 Nobel prizes were given for the years 1940–1942.
10   Different groups give out each award. The Royal Swedish Academy of
11 Sciences makes the physics and chemistry awards. The Karolinska Institute of
12 Stockholm, Sweden, awards the physiology or medicine prize. The Nobel Prize

13 for literature is awarded by the Swedish Academy. The Norwegian parliament
14 chooses a committee of five people to award the Nobel Peace Prize. In 1969,
15 a sixth prize was established in economics. The Royal Swedish Academy of
16 Sciences makes this award, too.

17 Each of these institutions must receive the names of candidates before
18 February 1 of each year. A jury of twelve people decides on a final candidate
19 by majority vote. If there is no majority vote for any one candidate, the prize
20 is not offered that year. The jury reviews the candidates and asks them many
21 questions, including the following:

22 • Did you make the outstanding contribution in the previous year?
23 • Was your contribution the result of many years of research?
24 • Did you work with one, two, or three scientists as a team? (The prize
25   may be divided.)
26 • Did your discovery depend on the work of another candidate? (Again,
27   the prize may be divided.)

28 The first Nobel prizes were awarded on December 10, 1901, the fifth
29 anniversary of Alfred Nobel's death. The amount of each prize was more
30 than $40,000 at that time. Today each prize is more than $1 million.

Questions for Another Look

1 _____ True _____ False   Each prize must be given out every year.

2 Why do you think no prizes were given out from 1940 to 1942?

_____

3 What happens if the jury of twelve people cannot agree on one candidate?

_____

4 Read the interview question again. "Did you make the outstanding
contribution in the previous year?" Why do you think this information
is important?

_____

Topics for Discussion and Writing

1. Pretend that you are wealthy. What do you want to happen to your property and money after you die? Write instructions.

2. Nominate a famous person for a Nobel Prize in one of the six categories. Describe the person and explain why you believe he or she deserves a Nobel Prize in that field.

3. Go to the library. Use an almanac to find the list of all the Nobel Prize winners. Select a Nobel Prize winner from any country in any field. Write about that man or woman, and why you think this person deserved the award.

4. Write a short biography of one of the Nobel Prize winners who interests you.

5. **Write in your journal.** Describe how you want people to remember you. Explain why you want people to remember you this way.

Follow-Up Activities

1. Work in groups of three or four. You are part of a committee that has to decide on a new category for the Nobel Prize. Remember, the fields now are physics, chemistry, medicine/physiology, literature, peace, and economics. Discuss the reasons why you think this seventh prize is a good idea. Compare your ideas with those of your classmates. Then take a vote to decide on the new category.

_____

_____

_____

_____

_____

_____

2 Work in groups of three or four. You are part of a committee that has to decide to eliminate one category from the Nobel Prize awards. Discuss the reasons you think this prize is no longer necessary or desirable. Compare your reasons with those of the class. Take a vote to decide on which category to eliminate.

_____

_____

_____

3 Go online. Search for a website that lists all the Nobel Prize winners. Make a list of the Nobel Prize winners from your country and/or another country you are interested in. Write down the year the people received their prize, and the field they received the prize in. Then choose one person and write about his or her achievement.

_____

_____

_____

_____

_____

_____

_____

_____

_____

_____

_____

_____

_____

_____

_____

_____

Word Search

Read the words listed below. Find them in the puzzle and circle them. They may be written in any direction.

annual	dangerous	honor	peaceful
award	explosives	information	powerful
construct	headlines	leader	remember

```
U   P   C   B   Q   O   J   G   S   Z   I   N   P   E   R
G   R   E   B   M   E   M   E   R   N   E   X   O   Q   Q
X   Q   T   R   I   G   N   I   F   W   K   V   W   U   X
K   M   S   E   V   I   S   O   L   P   X   E   E   K   Y
M   S   T   U   L   R   R   B   A   N   M   H   R   P   Y
S   X   C   D   O   M   P   T   U   N   I   L   F   M   R
F   H   A   N   A   R   G   A   V   R   N   V   U   F   L
S   E   O   T   P   P   E   A   C   E   F   U   L   E   L
H   H   I   Z   D   J   Q   G   L   M   P   H   A   V   F
N   O   T   C   U   R   T   S   N   O   C   D   H   L   E
N   U   O   K   M   C   A   P   M   A   E   S   L   R   F
S   T   F   J   C   S   N   W   B   R   D   M   K   H   S
O   K   Y   L   K   S   O   C   A   X   F   I   D   D   Q
```

Crossword Puzzle

Read the clues on the next page. Write the answers in the correct spaces in the puzzle.

Crossword Puzzle Clues

1. You and I
2. I spoke to John yesterday. _____ mother is visiting him.
4. Alfred Nobel's _____ was Swedish.
5. I don't want people to forget me. I want them to _____ me.
7. Laura and I like _____ class.
9. _____ is the explosive that made Nobel rich.
11. Bombs, guns, and tanks are powerful _____.
12. Bombs are _____. They blow up when they hit something.
16. The Nobel Prize is an _____ for a person's achievements.
17. Nobel hated fighting and war. He hated all kinds of _____.
19. Nine million dollars is a lot of money. To some people it is a _____.
21. Error

1. A _____ states how a person wishes his or her possessions to be distributed after death.
2. A _____ is the title of a newspaper article.
3. Alfred Nobel wanted to _____, or create, an explosive that was safe to use.
6. I have _____ pen. Do you have your pen?
8. Disturbed
9. Unsafe
10. Chemistry is a _____ of study.
13. The opposite of **war**
14. Certain
15. Build
18. **I, you, _____ she, it**
20. I called Sam on the phone. I spoke to _____ for a short time.

Grammar Cloze Quiz

Read the passage below. Complete each blank space with the simple past tense of one of the verbs listed. You may use the verbs more than once.

be	have	make	think
become	know	read	write

    After Nobel _____ the newspaper story, he _____ very upset

(1)   (2)

about the image that the world _____ of him. He _____ about
(3)   (4)

his problem for years. Then in 1895, an adventurer named Salomon August

Andree _____ plans to reach the North Pole. People all over the world
(5)

_____ excited about Andree's journey. Nobel _____ about
(6)   (7)

Andree's plan, too, and _____ an inspiration. He finally _____
(8)   (9)

what to do with his fortune, and he _____ his Last Will and Testament
(10)

to give instructions for his plan.

    Alfred Nobel died on December 10, 1896. He _____ unmarried,
(11)

and had no children. People all over the world _____ amazed when
(12)

they _____ in the newspapers about Alfred Nobel's plan. However,
(13)

after his death, the Nobel Prize _____ the greatest honor a person
(14)

could achieve.

Marie Curie:
Nobel Prize Winner

Prereading Preparation

1 Look at the photograph of Marie Curie, who was a Nobel Prize winner.

a. What was Marie Curie's profession?

1. She was a doctor.
2. She was a scientist.
3. She was an inventor.

b. What kind of work did Marie Curie do?

1. She helped sick people.
2. She invented new chemicals.
3. She did research.

c. Where did Marie Curie do most of her work?

1. In a laboratory
2. In a hospital
3. In an office

2 Look at the title of the chapter. What do you think Marie Curie won the Nobel Prize for?

a. Economics
b. Physics
c. Chemistry
d. Medicine
e. Peace
f. Literature

3 How many times do you think Marie Curie won a Nobel Prize?

a. Once
b. Twice
c. Three times

Track 19

Marie Curie: Nobel Prize Winner

1   Marya Sklodowska was born on November 7, 1867, in Poland. Marya's father
2 wanted his five children to become well educated. Unfortunately, the family was
3 poor. In fact, Marya worked for six years to support her older sister Bronya so
4 Bronya could study medicine at the Sorbonne in Paris. When Bronya finished
5 medical school in 1891, 23-year-old Marya Sklodowska went to Paris to begin
6 her own education.
7   Once she arrived in Paris, Marya changed her name to the French form,
8 Marie. After living with Bronya and her husband for a short time, she moved
9 to an inexpensive apartment near the university so she could study without
10 interruption. Marie's student life was extremely poor, but in spite of her difficult
11 living conditions, she was happy.
12   In July 1893, Marie passed her physics examination, first in her class. At
13 this time, she met Pierre Curie, a young scientist. Marie and Pierre discovered
14 that they had much in common. They both believed that science was the most
15 important part of their lives. They didn't care about money or about being
16 comfortable. They fell in love, and were married on July 26, 1895. Marie and
17 Pierre Curie were very happy. They discussed their work and the latest scientific
18 events, such as the discovery of X-rays.[1] Marie was interested in this research,

---

[1]X-rays: An invisible, high-energy form of light that can pass through many solid objects, such as the human body.

UNIT 5   INTERNATIONAL SCIENTISTS

and began to look for unknown elements that had such rays. Pierre Curie stopped his own research in order to help Marie in her work. He realized that she was about to make an important discovery.

In 1898, the Curies discovered two new elements that give off radiation. They named these elements polonium and radium. In those days, no one knew that such radioactive materials were dangerous. In fact, Marie Curie created the word *radioactive* to describe these materials. They did not know that exposure to this radioactivity caused their constant fatigue and illnesses, and they kept working. Finally, in 1902, they proved the existence of radium.

On June 25, 1903, Marie became the first woman to receive a doctor of science degree from the Sorbonne. Then she received an even greater award. In 1903, the Academy of Science at Stockholm, Sweden awarded the Nobel Prize in Physics to Marie and Pierre Curie and Henri Becquerel for their discoveries in radioactivity.

The Curies continued to work closely together until a tragic event occurred. On a rainy day in April, 1906, Pierre was killed in a street accident. Marie was heartbroken, but she continued working. Then, in 1910, she isolated radium. It was the biggest accomplishment of Marie Curie's career. In 1911, she received the Nobel Prize again, this time in Chemistry. She was the first woman to receive the Nobel Prize, and the first person to receive it a second time.

Over the years, Marie's constant exposure to radiation continued to destroy her health. She died on July 4, 1934, from an illness caused by her life's work: radium. Marie Curie never cared about making any money from her discoveries. Her life had been one of hard work, perseverance, and self-sacrifice. However, in her personal life, she was happily married and had two daughters. Professionally, she made important discoveries and achieved greatness in her field.

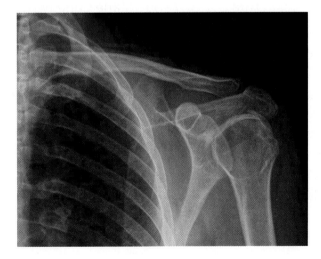

Fact-Finding Exercise

Read the passage once. Then read the following statements. Check whether they are True or False. If a statement is false, rewrite it so that it is true. Then go back to the passage and find the line that supports your answer.

1 _____ True _____ False Marie Curie was Marya Sklodowska.

_____

2 _____ True _____ False Marie Curie was born in Paris.

_____

3 _____ True _____ False Marie went to the University of Poland.

_____

4 _____ True _____ False Marie's husband, Pierre, was a scientist.

_____

5 _____ True _____ False The Curies discovered two new elements.

_____

6 _____ True _____ False Radium made the Curies feel tired and sick.

_____

7 _____ True _____ False Marie Curie was the first person to receive the Nobel Prize.

_____

8 _____ True _____ False Marie Curie won the Nobel Prize twice.

_____

9 _____ True _____ False Marie Curie wanted to earn a lot of money.

_____

Skimming and Scanning Exercise

Skim through the passage. Then read the following statements. Choose the one that is the correct main idea of the reading.

    a. Marie Curie discovered two new elements, polonium and radium.
    b. Marie Curie was a great scientist who won the Nobel Prize twice.
    c. Marie Curie did research on radioactive materials for many years.

Scan the passage. Work with a partner. Look at the time line below for Marie Curie's life. Choose ten important dates in her life. Then fill in the time line with the years you have chosen. On the lines below, write a sentence to describe what important event happened for each date.

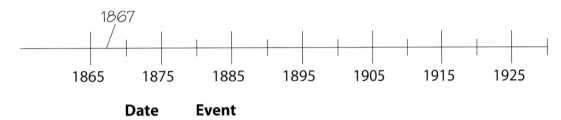

1867

1865   1875   1885   1895   1905   1915   1925

Date   **Event**

Example: *1867—Marie Curie was born.*

1. _____

2. _____

3. _____

4. _____

5. _____

6. _____

7. _____

8. _____

9. _____

10. _____

Reading Analysis

Read each question carefully. Either circle the letter or the number of the correct answer or write your answer in the space provided.

1 Marya's father wanted his five children to become well educated. **Unfortunately,** the family was poor.

   a. How many brothers and sisters did Marya have? _____

   b. This sentence means that

      1. none of the children went to a university
      2. all the children went to a university
      3. the family could not afford to send the children to a university

   c. Complete the following sentence with the correct choice. Marie and Pierre Curie worked well together for many years.

   Unfortunately,

      1. Pierre died when he was still young
      2. Pierre and Marie discovered two new elements
      3. Pierre and Marie shared the Nobel Prize in 1903

2 The family was poor. **In fact,** Marya **supported** her older sister Bronya until she finished medical school at the **Sorbonne** in Paris.

   a. This sentence means that

      1. Marya lived with her sister
      2. Marya gave her sister money to live on
      3. Marya helped her sister study

   b. What information follows **in fact?**

      1. Additional information that gives more details about the previous sentence
      2. Different information that introduces a new idea

   c. The **Sorbonne** is

      1. a business
      2. a hospital
      3. a school

3 **Once** she arrived in Paris, Marya changed her name to the French form, Marie.

In this context, **once** means

   a. one time
   b. when
   c. before

4 Marya's student life was very poor, but **in spite of** her **difficult living conditions,** she was happy.

   a. This sentence means that

      1. Marya's living conditions made her happy because they were difficult

      2. Marya's living conditions were bad, but she was happy

   b. Read the following sentences. Write **in spite of** in the appropriate sentence.

      1. John was very sick. _____ his illness, he went to work.

      2. John was very sick. _____ his illness, he went to the hospital.

   c. **Difficult living conditions** refers to the fact that

      1. Marya lived in a cold, uncomfortable apartment and ate little food

      2. Marya was a student and had to study hard

5 In July 1893, Marie passed her physics exam, **first in her class. At this time,** she met Pierre Curie, a young scientist.

   a. What does **first in her class** mean?

      1. Marie graduated before all the other students.

      2. Marie was the best student in her class.

   b. **At this time** means

      1. at the same time she passed her exam

      2. in the 1890s

      3. during this time period

6 Marie and Pierre Curie discussed their work and the latest scientific events, such as the discovery of **X-rays.**

   a. What are **X-rays?**

   _____

   _____

   b. How do you know?

   _____

   _____

   c. This kind of information is called a

   _____

   _____

7 Pierre Curie stopped his own research **in order to** help Marie.

    a. Pierre Curie stopped his own research
        1. because he wanted to help Marie
        2. because he wanted to tell Marie what to do

    b. What follows **in order to?**
        1. An example
        2. A result
        3. A reason

8 Pierre realized that Marie was **about to** make an important discovery. **About to** means

    a. the time immediately before something happens
    b. the time immediately after something happens
    c. at the moment something is happening

9 In 1898, the Curies discovered two new elements that give off radiation. They named these elements polonium and radium. In those days, no one knew that **such radioactive materials** were dangerous.

What does **such radioactive materials** refer to?

_____

10 Marie Curie created the term **radioactivity** to describe these materials. This sentence means that

    a. Marie Curie was the first person to use the word _radioactivity_
    b. Marie Curie invented these radioactive materials

11 The Curies continued to work closely together **until** a **tragic** event occurred. On a rainy day in April, 1906, Pierre was killed in a street accident. Marie was **heartbroken,** but she continued working.

    a. **Until** means
        1. up to the time when something else happens
        2. up to the time when something else finishes

b. Read the following sentences. Write the word **until** in the appropriate sentence.

    1. John studied very hard _____ he finished the exam.
    2. John studied very hard _____ the exam began.

c. The word **tragic** means

    1. very violent
    2. very sad
    3. very surprising

d. **Heartbroken** means that

    1. Marie was very unhappy
    2. Marie became very sick

12 **Over the years,** Marie's constant exposure to radiation continued to destroy her health.

Over the years means

a. in the years immediately before Marie died
b. through all the years that she worked

13 Marie Curie's life had been one of hard work, **perseverance,** and self-sacrifice. However, in her personal life she was happy, and professionally, she achieved greatness in her **field.**

a. Think about Marie Curie's life. What does the characteristic of **perseverance** mean?

    1. Marie Curie had a sad life.
    2. Marie Curie never stopped trying.
    3. Marie Curie had little money.

b. What was Marie Curie's **field?**

    1. Paris
    2. Career
    3. Science

Dictionary Skills

Read the dictionary entry for each word and think about the context of the sentence. Write the number of the appropriate definition on the line next to the word. Then choose the sentence with the correct answer.

 support *v.* [T] **1** to hold up or bear the weight of: *a beam that supports a ceiling* **2** to provide the money for necessities of life: *She supports her family by working two jobs.* **3** to contribute to; to encourage and assist by giving money to or working for: *We support our local hospital by giving blood regularly.* **4** to agree with, advocate, or express loyalty to: *He supports our efforts to end hunger in the world.*

Marya **supported** her older sister Bronya for six years while Bronya studied medicine at the Sorbonne in Paris.

a. support: _____
b. 1. Marya worked with Bronya while Bronya studied medicine at the Sorbonne.
   2. Marya provided Bronya with money to live on while Bronya studied medicine at the Sorbonne.

 interrupt *v.* [T] **1** to stop s.t. from continuing: *A bad storm interrupted telephone communications between the two islands.* **2** to start talking or doing s.t. in the middle of s.o.'s conversation or activity, to break in: *Our little boy always interrupts our conversations by asking questions.* -*n.* [C; U] **interruption.**

After living with Bronya and her husband for a short time, Marie moved to an inexpensive apartment near the university, so no one would **interrupt** her while she studied.

a. interrupt: _____
b. 1. Marie moved to an inexpensive apartment, so no one would talk to her or disturb her while she studied.
   2. Marie moved to an inexpensive apartment, so no one could stop her from studying.

3 constant *adj.* **1** happening all the time, continuous: *I can't sleep because of the constant noise of the cars and trucks on the street.* **2** unchanging: *For 15 years, I have had a constant problem with a bad back.* **3** *frml.* faithful: *He is constant in his love for her.*

—*n.* **1** a quantity or quality that does not change: *In Rhode Island, the speed limit is a constant at 55 miles per hour.* **2** a quantity in a mathematical equation or expression that has a fixed value and no variable: *In the equation $y = 3x + 5$, the number 5 is a constant. -adv.* **constantly**

Marie's **constant** exposure to radiation over so many years eventually caused her death.

a. **constant:** _____ (adjective / noun)
b. 1. Marie's unchanging exposure to radiation eventually caused her death.
   2. Marie's faithful exposure to radiation eventually caused her death.
   3. Marie's continuous exposure to radiation eventually caused her death.

4 exposure *n.* **1** [C; U] being unprotected, esp. from cold weather: *The lost mountain climbers suffered from exposure.* **2** [U] risk of loss: *We limit our exposure by investing only one quarter of the money.* **3** [C] a section of photographic film: *That roll of film contains 36 exposures.* **4** [C] a position or view in relation to a direction on the compass (north, south, east, or west): *The living room has a southern exposure.*

Marie's death was caused by her constant **exposure** to radiation over so many years.

a. **exposure:** _____
b. 1. Marie's death was caused by her risk of loss from radiation over so many years.
   2. Marie's death was caused by her constantly being unprotected from radiation over so many years.
   3. Marie's death was caused by her position in relation to radiation over so many years.

Word Forms

In English, some verbs become nouns by adding the suffixes -ance or -ence, for example, persist (v.), persistence (n.). Complete each sentence with the correct form of the word on the left. Be careful of spelling changes. **Write all the verbs in the past tense. The verbs may be affirmative or negative. The nouns may be singular or plural.**

occur (v.)

occurrence (n.)

1 Janet experienced several _____ of a serious illness before she began to get well. Finally, she felt well, her illness _____ again, and she was very happy.

exist (v.)

existence (n.)

2 After years of hard work, Marie and Pierre Curie proved the _____ of radium. No one knew that radium _____ until they discovered it.

persevere (v.)

perseverance (n.)

3 Henry was having a lot of trouble learning calculus, and he _____ because he became discouraged. Because he had no _____, he gave up and failed his exams.

assist (v.)

assistance (n.)

4 When Andrew registered for classes, he needed some _____. Unfortunately, no one _____ him, and he filled out all the forms incorrectly.

assure (v.)

assurance (n.)

5 My brother Edward _____ me enough that plane travel is safe. Although he gave me many _____, I was very frightened on my first plane trip.

In English, some adjectives become nouns by adding the suffix -ness, for example, *sick (adj.), sickness (n.)*. Complete each sentence with the correct form of the words on the left. **The nouns may be singular or plural.**

great *(adj.)*

greatness *(n.)*

1 Natalie has a reputation as a ＿＿＿＿＿＿ tennis player. She has won many international competitions, and news of her ＿＿＿＿＿＿ is spreading around the world.

happy *(adj.)*

happiness *(n.)*

2 Alex and Victoria's ＿＿＿＿＿＿ is not accidental. They get along well, they have jobs they like, and they live in a comfortable home. Naturally, they are very ＿＿＿＿＿＿ with their lives.

short *(adj.)*

shortness *(n.)*

3 It is a very ＿＿＿＿＿＿ distance between Larry's house and the health club. It's just a five-minute walk. The ＿＿＿＿＿＿ of the trip makes it convenient for Larry to exercise there every day.

near *(adj.)*

nearness *(n.)*

4 The shopping center is quite ＿＿＿＿＿＿ Shirley's house. Because of the center's ＿＿＿＿＿＿ to her home, she walks there to go shopping.

ill *(adj.)*

illness *(n.)*

5 It seems that Beverly is always ＿＿＿＿＿＿. In fact, she has had four different ＿＿＿＿＿＿ so far this year.

Word Partnership	Use *ill* with:
v.	become ill, feel ill, look ill
adv.	critically ill, mentally ill, physically ill, seriously ill, very ill

Vocabulary in Context

assured *(v.)*	exposure *(n.)*	occurred *(v.)*	perseverance *(n.)*
constant *(adj.)*	in spite of	once	tragic *(adj.)*

Read the following sentences. Complete each blank space with the correct word or phrase from the list above. Use each word or phrase only once.

1. _____ the long distance between Jane's home and the store, Jane decided to walk instead of taking the bus.

2. Thomas is well known for his _____. He never gives up, no matter how difficult a job is, or how long it might take.

3. The policeman asked how the accident _____. The driver told him that her car slipped on the ice and hit a tree.

4. My grandfather's dog is his _____ companion. It goes with him wherever he goes.

5. _____ you complete the application form, you can take the entrance exam.

6. The fire in John's home was a _____ accident. He and his wife were very badly burned.

7. Marta _____ the lost child that she would help him find his parents, and he stopped crying.

8. Constant _____ to the sun can result in skin cancer. Be sure to use sunscreen.

Think About It

Read the following questions and think about the answers. Write your answer below each question. Then compare your answers with those of your classmates.

1 Marie Curie postponed, or delayed, her own education for six years so her older sister Bronya could attend medical school. Why do you think she did this?

_____

_____

_____

2 How did Bronya repay Marie for Marie's support?

_____

_____

_____

3 What kind of woman was Marie Curie? Write some adjectives that describe her.

_____

_____

_____

4 Marie Curie never cared about making money. As a result, she sometimes worked under hard conditions. Do you agree with her philosophy? Explain your reasons.

_____

_____

_____

Another Look

Read the following passage about Irene Curie, Marie and Pierre Curie's daughter. Then answer the questions that follow.

Track 20

Irene Curie

1   Most people are aware that Marie Curie was the first woman to win the
2   Nobel Prize, and the first person to win it twice. However, few people know
3   that Marie Curie was also the mother of a Nobel Prize winner. Irene Curie was
4   born on September 12, 1897. Irene was the first of Marie and Pierre Curie's two
5   daughters. At the age of ten, Irene's talents and interest in mathematics were
6   apparent. Irene, along with nine other children whose parents were also famous
7   scholars, studied in their own school. It was known as the "Cooperative," and
8   Marie Curie was one of their teachers. Irene finished her high school education
9   at the College of Sevigne in Paris.
10   Irene entered the Sorbonne in October 1914 to prepare for a degree in mathematics
11   and physics. When World War I began, Irene left the Sorbonne to help her mother,
12   who was using X-ray facilities to help save the lives of wounded soldiers. Irene
13   continued this work by developing X-ray facilities in military hospitals in France and
14   Belgium. After the war, Irene received a Military Medal for her work.
15   In 1918, Irene became her mother's assistant at the Curie Institute. In
16   December 1924, Frederic Joliot visited the Institute, where he met Marie Curie.
17   Frederic became one of Marie's assistants, and Irene taught him the techniques
18   required to work with radioactivity. Irene and Frederic soon fell in love and were
19   married on October 29, 1926. Their daughter Helene was born on September 17,
20   1927, and their son Pierre on March 12, 1932. Like her mother, Irene combined
21   family and career. Like her mother, Irene was awarded a Nobel Prize, along
22   with her husband Frederic, in 1935, for synthesizing new radioactive elements.
23   Unfortunately, also like her mother, she developed leukemia because of her
24   exposure to radiation. Irene Joliot-Curie died from leukemia on March 17, 1956.

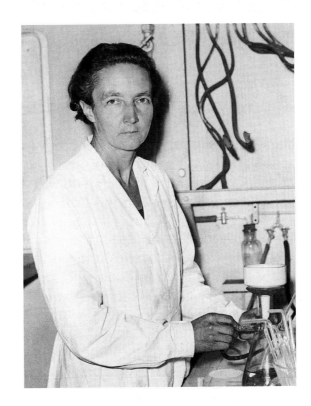

Questions for Another Look

1 How was Irene Curie's education unusual?

_____

_____

2 Where did Irene meet her husband?

_____

_____

3 Why did Irene receive a Military Medal for her work?
   a. Because she did scientific research
   b. Because she helped the wounded soldiers
   c. Because she received a degree in mathematics

4 Describe two ways that Irene and her mother, Marie Curie, were similar.

_____

_____

_____

Topics for Discussion and Writing

1   **a.**   Who wins Nobel Prizes?

      b.   What types of work or discoveries deserve a Nobel Prize?

2   Marie Curie supported her sister Bronya when Bronya was in medical school. Then, when Bronya finished school, Marie began her own education. What kind of person do you think she was? Would you support your sister or brother if you could? Explain your reasons.

3   Marie Curie made a lot of sacrifices for her work. She never made any money from her discoveries, and died from her life's work: radium. Do you know of any other individuals who sacrificed their lives for their work? Do you think you could sacrifice your life for your work? Why or why not? Explain your reasons.

4   Write your autobiography or the biography of someone you know personally and whom you admire.

5   **Write in your journal.** Work was the most important part of Marie Curie's life. Describe the most important part of your life at the present time. What do you think the most important part of your life will be in the future. Why?

Follow-Up Activities

1 Go online and search for more information about Marie and Pierre's younger daughter, Eve. For example, when was she born? What did she do? Was she a scientist, too? Did she become well-known, too? Share your information with the class.

_____

_____

_____

_____

_____

2 A biography is the story of a person's life. Prepare a biography of an important person from your country. Give an oral presentation to your class.

_____

_____

_____

_____

_____

3 Work in pairs or small groups. Make a list of the five most important discoveries of the twentieth century. Remember, a discovery is something a person _finds_, something that exists. An invention is something a person _creates_, such as the telephone, the light bulb, the automobile. Combine your list with the other groups' lists. Together, choose the three most important discoveries.

_____

_____

_____

_____

_____

Word Search

Read the words listed below. Find them in the puzzle and circle them. They may be written in any direction.

achieve	exposure	perseverance	support
discovery	field	radium	tragic
existence	heartbroken	scientist	unfortunately

```
D  B  D  C  S  L  B  E  N  D  V  L  U  X  T
H  T  C  U  U  E  X  I  S  T  E  N  C  E  T
D  B  F  M  P  T  A  V  H  P  F  H  J  Z  O
X  S  I  M  P  E  R  U  S  O  P  X  E  U  Z
Z  N  E  K  O  R  B  T  R  A  E  H  A  R  O
P  F  L  H  R  Q  E  T  Y  V  X  H  B  D  H
F  N  D  T  T  J  U  V  R  V  M  S  U  J  Z
N  O  X  E  C  N  A  R  E  V  E  S  R  E  P
Q  C  N  O  A  D  O  D  V  I  Y  J  V  D  Q
K  U  M  T  R  W  N  Q  O  U  H  O  T  C  Y
X  F  E  F  A  J  O  X  C  D  S  C  R  X  N
W  L  E  X  D  T  X  B  S  L  B  T  A  W  M
Y  R  S  C  I  E  N  T  I  S  T  Y  G  X  L
T  F  T  S  U  H  Y  X  D  I  Q  B  I  Y  N
X  P  Y  G  M  M  C  I  D  O  S  L  C  C  T
```

Crossword Puzzle

Read the clues on the next page. Write the answers in the correct spaces in the puzzle.

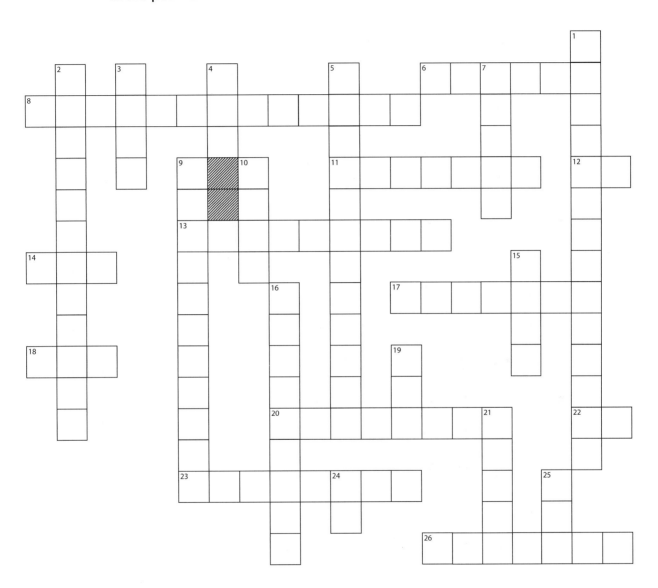

Crossword Puzzle Clues

6. A death is a very _____ occurrence.
8. Unhappily; unluckily
11. Give someone money to help him or her live or go to school
12. I, _____; he, him
13. When you find something for the first time, you make a _____.
14. Past participle of **put**
17. Sickness
18. Past participle of **hit**
20. Polonium, radium, gold, and iron are all _____.
22. The opposite of **yes**
23. _____ to X-rays or to the sun's rays can cause injury to the body.
26. After a long time

1. Achievement
2. Something that causes a break in your work is an _____.
3. Past participle of **go**
4. Past participle of **run**
5. If you do not give up easily, you have _____.
7. The Nobel Prize is an important _____.
9. Polonium, radium, uranium, and plutonium are all _____ elements.
10. Past participle of **lose**
15. Past participle of **lend**
16. Harmful
19. _____, two, three, four
21. Past participle of **show**
24. The opposite of **down**
25. Every

Grammar Cloze Quiz

Read the passage. Complete each blank space with one of the pronouns listed below. You may use the pronouns more than once.

he	his	their
her	she	they

In 1891, 23-year-old Marya Sklodowska went to Paris to begin _____ (1) education. Once _____ (2) arrived in Paris, Marya changed _____ (3) name to the French form, Marie. After living with Bronya and _____ (4) husband for a short time, _____ (5) moved near the university so _____ (6) could study without interruption. Marie's student life was extremely poor, but in spite of _____ (7) difficult living conditions, _____ (8) was happy.

In July 1893, Marie passed _____ (9) physics examination, first in _____ (10) class. At this time _____ (11) met Pierre Curie. _____ (12) was a young scientist. Marie and Pierre discovered that _____ (13) had much in common. _____ (14) both believed that science was the most important part of _____ (15) lives. _____ (16) fell in love and were married on July 26, 1895.

Marie and Pierre Curie were very happy. _____ (17) discussed _____ (18) work and the latest scientific events. Marie began to do research on X-rays. Pierre Curie stopped _____ (19) own research in order to help Marie in _____ (20) work. _____ (21) realized that _____ (22) was about to make an important discovery.

1. Marie Curie won two Nobel Prizes for her achievements in science. Do you think Marie Curie's work agrees with Alfred Nobel's idea of special achievement? Explain your answer.

   _____

   _____

   _____

   _____

   _____

   _____

2. Would you like to win a Nobel Prize? How? In what category? Nobel Prize winners receive approximately $1.5 million in prize money. What would you do with the money?

   _____

   _____

   _____

   _____

   _____

   _____

The Earth's Resources and Dangers

11 CHAPTER

Oil as an Important World Resource

Prereading Preparation

1 Work with a partner to make a list of some uses of oil for the home and transportation.

USES OF OIL	
Transportation	Home

2 Look at the illustration below. Then read the paragraph on the next page. Complete the flowchart on page 223, using information from both.

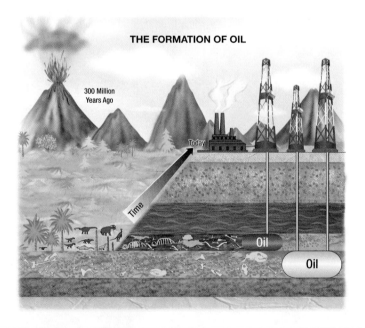

THE FORMATION OF OIL

300 Million Years Ago

Today

Time

Oil

Oil

The Formation of Oil

Oil is usually called petroleum. Petroleum is very complex, but it is made up of only two elements: carbon (C) and hydrogen (H). Together, carbon and hydrogen are called hydrocarbons. Hydrocarbons are the remains of ancient plants and animals. These plants and animals lived and died millions of years ago. When they died, they were covered by mud, and bacteria broke down the organic remains. Over thousands of years, more plants and animals died and were covered by more mud. The weight of the upper layers and the heat from the pressure eventually changed the mud into solid rock, called sedimentary rock. It also changed the organic material into oil and natural gas.

FLOWCHART: THE FORMATION OF OIL

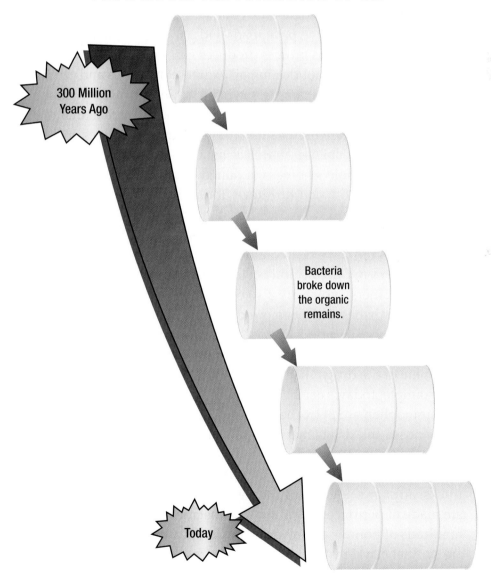

300 Million Years Ago

Bacteria broke down the organic remains.

Today

Oil as an Important World Resource

1   We may not realize it, but oil is an essential part of our everyday lives. Oil, which
2   is usually called petroleum, is a valuable world resource because of the many
3   useful products that are manufactured from it. In fact, petroleum is probably the
4   most important substance we use in modern society, next to water. The process of
5   manufacturing petroleum products begins when oil is first taken out of the ground.

6   When petroleum first comes out of the ground, it is called crude oil. This oil is
7   impure. In other words, it is dirty and people need to clean, or refine, it. First, the
8   oil goes into a furnace to heat it. When the oil is heated, it separates into lighter and
9   heavier parts. For example, the lightest part of the oil becomes natural gas. We use
10 natural gas to heat our homes and cook with. The heaviest part of the oil becomes
11 asphalt. We use asphalt to pave roads and parking lots. In between the natural
12 gas and the asphalt, this process produces gasoline, kerosene, heating oil, and
13 lubricating oil. We use lubricating oil to grease machines and other metal objects
14 with moving parts, for example, sewing machines. However, these are just a few of
15 the 6,000 petroleum products, or petrochemicals, that are manufactured from crude
16 oil. Petrochemicals are used in almost every area of our lives, including housing,
17 clothing, and personal use, as well as medicine and transportation.

18 In the past, people's homes contained only natural materials, such as wool or
19 cotton carpets, and wood furniture. Today, however, furniture, furniture fabrics,
20 carpeting, paint, and wallpaper are all made from petroleum-based synthetics.
21 We heat our homes with oil or natural gas instead of wood. In the past 50
22 years our clothes have been made from synthetic fibers such as rayon, nylon,
23 polyester, Orlon, Dacron, and acetate. Today, clothing is even made from used
24 plastic containers, which are also petrochemical products. The detergents we
25 use to wash dishes and clean our clothes are petroleum-based products, as are
26 children's toys, shampoo, lipstick, and hand lotion.

27 Petrochemicals have a wide variety of medical uses. The vitamins we take
28 and some of the drugs that our doctors prescribe are made of petrochemicals.
29 For example, today's aspirin and other synthetic pain relievers such as
30 acetaminophen are petrochemical products. Cold medicines that relieve our
31 stuffy noses and drugs that help some people breathe more easily are, too.

32 The transportation industry is very dependent on petrochemicals. We all
33 know that gasoline, kerosene, and diesel oil provide fuel for cars, motorcycles,
34 trucks, airplanes, and ships. However, not everyone is aware that cars and trucks
35 are made of petrochemicals, too. For instance, car and truck bodies are made of
36 hundreds of pounds of polyester. Bumpers are no longer made of steel, and tires
37 are synthetic, not real, rubber. Seat covers are vinyl. Traffic lights, road signs, and
38 the painted lines on roads are all made of petrochemicals.

39
40
41

Although the world supply of petroleum is limited and will run out one day, for now we have an adequate supply to meet the world's needs. Petrochemical products will remain an essential part of our lives for many years to come.

OIL DRILLING AND REFINING PROCESS

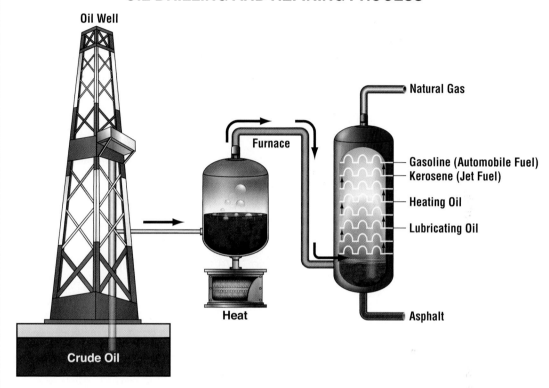

Fact-Finding Exercise

Read the passage once. Then read the following statements. Check whether they are True or False. If a statement is false, rewrite it so that it is true. Then go back to the passage and find the line that supports your answer.

1 _____ True _____ False   Petroleum is another word for oil.

_____

2 _____ True _____ False   Crude oil does not need to be cleaned.

_____

3 _____ True _____ False   The lightest part of the oil becomes natural gas.

_____

4 _____ True _____ False   Kerosene is heavier than asphalt.

_____

5 _____ True _____ False   Our homes contain many products made
of petrochemicals.

_____

6 _____ True _____ False   Petrochemicals have no medical uses.

_____

7 _____ True _____ False   We all use and depend on petroleum products.

_____

B Skimming and Scanning Exercise

PART 1

Skim through the passage. Then read the following statements. Choose the one
that is the correct main idea of the reading.

a. Petroleum is dirty when it comes from the ground and needs
to be cleaned.
b. Heating crude oil separates it into lighter and heavier parts.
c. Petroleum is an important natural resource that has many
essential uses.

Scan the passage. Work with a partner to fill in the chart with information from the reading.

USES OF PETROLEUM					
Housing	Clothing	Personal Uses	Medical Uses	Transportation	Other Uses

Reading Analysis

Read each question carefully. Either circle the letter or the number of the correct answer or write your answer in the space provided.

1 Oil, which is usually called **petroleum,** is a valuable world resource because of the many useful products that are manufactured from it. **In fact,** petroleum is probably the most important substance we use in modern society, **next to** water.

  a. What is a synonym for **petroleum?**

    _____

  b. The sentence after **in fact**

    1. is the same as the sentence before it, but in different words
    2. emphasizes the information before it
    3. is a different idea from the information before it

  c. Complete the following sentence with the appropriate choice. Yesterday was a very cold day. **In fact,**

    1. I had to wear a heavy coat
    2. it snowed all day long
    3. the temperature was 10°F below zero

  d. Petroleum is the most important substance we use in modern society, **next to** water.

    In modern society, which substance is the most important: petroleum or water?

    _____

2 When petroleum first comes out of the ground, it is called crude oil. This oil is **impure. In other words,** it is dirty and people need to clean, or **refine**, it.

  a. What does **impure** mean?

    1. Oil
    2. Dirty
    3. From the ground

  b. What type of information follows **in other words?**

    1. An example
    2. Additional information
    3. The same information in different words

c. What does **refine** mean?

_____

d. How do you know?

_____

3 Gasoline, kerosene, and asphalt are just a few of the 6,000 petroleum products, or **petrochemicals,** that are manufactured from crude oil. Petrochemicals are used in almost every area of our lives, including housing, clothing, and personal use, **as well as** medicine and transportation.

a. What are **petrochemicals?**

_____

b. What does **as well as** mean?
   1. Very good
   2. Equal to
   3. In addition to

4 In the past, people's homes contained only **natural** materials, such as wool or cotton carpets, and wood furniture. Today, however, furniture, furniture fabrics, carpeting, paint, and wallpaper are all made from petroleum-based **synthetics.**

a. What are examples of **natural** materials?

_____

b. What are **synthetic** materials?
   1. Artificial; man-made
   2. Materials for home use

5 The **detergents** we use to wash dishes and clean our clothes are petroleum-based products, **as are** children's toys, shampoo, lipstick, and hand lotion.

a. **Detergent** is
   1. a kind of machine
   2. a kind of soap
   3. a kind of process

b. In this sentence, **as are** means
   1. children's toys, shampoo, lipstick, and hand lotion are petroleum-based products, too
   2. children's toys, shampoo, lipstick, and hand lotion are washed with detergent, too

6 Some of the drugs that our doctors **prescribe** are made of petrochemicals. For example, today's aspirin and other synthetic pain **relievers** such as acetaminophen are petrochemical products.

    a. When doctors **prescribe** medicine, they

        1. sell medicine to us
        2. make medicine for us
        3. order the use of a specific medicine

    b. A pain **reliever** is a drug that

        1. lessens our pain
        2. is synthetic

7 Car and truck **bodies** are made of hundreds of pounds of polyester. Car and truck **bodies** are

    a. people in cars and trucks
    b. the front, back, sides, and doors of cars and trucks
    c. people that cars and trucks hit and kill

8 Although the world supply of petroleum is limited, and will **run out** one day, for now we have an **adequate** supply to meet the world's needs. Petrochemical products will remain an essential part of our lives for many years to come.

    a. One day the world supply of petroleum

        1. will be part of our lives
        2. will not be necessary
        3. will end

    b. **Adequate** means

        1. expensive
        2. enough
        3. useful

Dictionary Skills

D

Read the dictionary entry for each word and think about the context of the sentence. Write the number of the appropriate definition on the line next to the word. In addition, circle *noun, adjective,* or *adverb* where indicated. Then choose the sentence with the correct answer.

1 **realize** *v.* [T] -ized, -izing, -izes **1** to understand, start to believe s.t. is true: *He realizes now that he needs to go back to college for more education.* **2** to gain, make money: *The woman realized a profit from the sale of her house.* **3** to make s.t. become true: *This summer I will realize my dream of going to Italy.*

We may not **realize** it, but oil is an essential part of our everyday lives. In fact, petroleum is the most important substance we use in modern society, next to water.

a. **realize:** _____
b. 1. We may not make any money from it, but oil is an essential part of our lives.
    2. We may not understand it, but oil is an essential part of our lives.
    3. We may not make it true, but oil is an essential part of our lives.

2 **essential** *adj.* **1** central, major: *The essential point is we must do what the contract says.* **2** necessary, required: *It is essential that you deliver the message this morning.*
—*n.pl.* **the essentials:** the things necessary to s.t.: *The essentials of life are food, shelter, and clothing.*

We may not realize it, but oil is an **essential** part of our everyday lives. In fact, petrochemical products will remain an **essential** part of our lives for many years to come.

a. **essential:** _____ (adjective / noun)
b. 1. Oil is a major part of our everyday lives.
    2. Oil is a required part of our everyday lives.

3 **substance** *n.* **1** [U] anything one can touch: *This face cream is a white, sticky substance.* ‖ *Tires are made of rubber and other substances.* **2** usu. sing. [C; U] meaning, truth: *What she says has substance because of her knowledge and experience.* **3** [U] wealth, possessions: *The family owns a successful business; they are people of substance.*

Petroleum is the most important **substance** we use in modern society, next to water.

a. **substance:** _____

b. 1. Petroleum is the most important truth in modern society, next to water.
    2. Petroleum is the most important wealth in modern society, next to water.
    3. Petroleum is the most important material in modern society, next to water.

---

4 **wide** *adj.* **wider, widest** **1** related to the distance from side to side: *That table is three feet wide.* **2** with a great distance from side to side: *A long bridge crossed the wide river.* **3** large: *She can play a wide range of musical instruments: the piano, guitar, and trumpet.*

—*adv.* **1** completely, fully: *wide-open* ‖ *wide-awake* **2** **wide of the mark:**
a. away from the target: *The arrow missed the center; it was wide of the mark.*
b. *fig.* wrong, incorrect: *His answer to the question was wide of the mark.*

-suffix *-wide* extending over or all through an area: *The position of governor is a state-wide elective office.* -*adv.* **widely;** -*n.* **wideness.**

Petrochemicals have a **wide** variety of medical uses. For example, the vitamins we take and some of the drugs that our doctors prescribe are made of petrochemicals.

a. **wide:** _____ (adjective / adverb)

b. 1. Petrochemicals have an extensive variety of medical uses.
    2. Petrochemicals have a distant variety of medical uses.
    3. Petrochemicals have a side-to-side variety of medical uses.

---

5 **aware** *adj.* **1** conscious of, alert to: *He is out of the coma, but he can't speak. He is aware of people around him though.* **2** knowledgeable about, understanding of: *A newspaper reporter must be aware of current events.*

—*n.* [U] **awareness.**

We all know that gasoline, kerosene, and diesel oil provide fuel for cars, motorcycles, trucks, airplanes, and ships. However, not everyone is **aware** that cars and trucks are made of petrochemicals, too.

a. **aware:** _____

b. 1. Not everyone is conscious of the fact that cars and trucks are made of petrochemicals.
    2. Not everyone is knowledgeable of the fact that cars and trucks are made of petrochemicals.

E Word Forms

In English, some verbs become nouns by adding the suffix *-tion,* for example, *create (v.), creation (n.).* If the word ends in *e,* the *e* is dropped. Furthermore, sometimes the word changes in spelling. Complete each sentence with the correct form of the word on the left. **Write all the verbs in the simple present tense. They may be affirmative or negative. The nouns may be singular or plural.**

produce *(v.)*

production *(n.)*

1 Australia _____ very much petroleum or natural gas. In fact, Australia's yearly _____ of oil and gas is the lowest in the world.

prescribe *(v.)*

prescription *(n.)*

2 Doctors are the only people who can write _____ for certain drugs that can be dangerous. However, doctors _____ basic drugs such as aspirin. We can buy them without a prescription.

transport *(v.)*

transportation *(n.)*

3 Petroleum companies _____ oil by airplane. They ship oil in large tankers, or ships. The _____ of oil is also done by pipeline, for example, in the state of Alaska.

lubricate *(v.)*

lubrication *(n.)*

4 Monica takes good care of her bicycle. She carefully _____ the gears and the chain every month. She uses a high-quality oil for proper _____.

add *(v.)*

addition *(n.)*

5 Bill and Arthur always _____ the figures on their check when they eat in a restaurant. Occasionally a waiter makes mistakes when he does his _____, so Bill and Arthur like to make sure the total is correct.

In English, the noun form and the verb form of some words are the same, for example, *drill (v.), drill (n.)*. Complete each sentence with the correct form of the word on the left. Circle *(v.)* if you are using the verb or *(n.)* if you are using the noun form of each word. **Write all the verbs in the simple present tense. They may be affirmative or negative. The nouns may be singular or plural.**

grease

1 There are many different types of _____ for various
 *(v., n.)*

purposes. For example, whenever Fred works on his car,

he _____ different parts of the engine.
 *(v., n.)*

heat

2 In many countries of the world, people _____ their
 *(v., n.)*

homes with oil or gas. They use wood or coal instead.

The amount of _____ that a house gets is usually
 *(v., n.)*

controlled with an instrument called a thermostat.

process

3 Many _____ are involved in the oil-refining
 *(v., n.)*

industry. However, most oil companies _____ crude
 *(v., n.)*

oil in the same manner.

fuel

4 People _____ their cars with gasoline, but trucks
 *(v., n.)*

usually use diesel oil. Airplanes do not use either gasoline

or diesel. The _____ they use is kerosene or jet fuel.
 *(v., n.)*

supply

5 Many countries now _____ the world with natural
(v., n.)

gas and oil, but these reserves are limited. At some time in the

next 100 years, the world's entire _____ of oil and gas
(v., n.)

will end, and all countries will need other sources of energy.

Word Partnership	Use *supply* with:
n.	supply **electricity**, supply **equipment**, supply **information**
adj.	**abundant** supply, **large** supply, **limited** supply

F Vocabulary in Context

adequate *(adj.)*	**fuel** *(n.)*	**next to**	**substance** *(n.)*
as well as	**impure** *(adj.)*	**process** *(n.)*	**synthetic** *(adj.)*

Read the following sentences. Complete each blank space with the correct word or phrase from the list above. Use each word or phrase only once.

1 Gasoline and kerosene are two types of _____.

2 Grease is a very oily _____. You need a strong detergent to wash it off your hands.

3 Don't drink the water in that river. It is _____. Drink the bottled water you have with you instead.

4 Making good coffee is a very simple _____. All you need is fresh cold water and the right amount of coffee.

5 I have an _____ number of chairs for all the people I have invited to my party. I don't need any more.

6 Today, many objects are made of _____ materials. Many of these materials are produced from petrochemicals.

7 I read books for pleasure _____ for information. Both are important to me.

8 _____ chocolate cake, my favorite dessert is ice cream.

G

Think About It

Read the following questions and think about the answers. Write your answer below each question. Then compare your answers with those of your classmates.

1 Besides oil, what is another valuable natural resource that is essential to our lives? Why is this natural resource essential?

_____

_____

_____

2 How do you think everyday life in the past was different without oil? Was it easier or more difficult? Explain your answer.

_____

_____

_____

3 What are other sources of energy that people can use instead of oil?

_____

_____

_____

H

Another Look

Read the following story, and then answer the questions.

Track 22

The Do It Homestead

1　　Charlie and Fran Collins live in southwest Utah on the family farm
2　which they built together. For the last 21 years, the Collinses have not
3　paid any electrical bills. They have run their home and their farm completely
4　on solar energy. They do not depend on electrical companies to supply
5　their power.
6　　Many people dream of becoming energy self-sufficient for different reasons.
7　Some people want to use energy sources that are safer for the environment,
8　or environmentally friendly. However, while most of us only dream about
9　becoming energy self-sufficient, Charlie and Fran Collins actually did it. When
10　the Collinses bought their 240-acre farm, they began experimenting with various
11　sources of light and energy. After 21 years, they have a lifestyle that has all of
12　the modern conveniences, but which is powered entirely on solar energy. The
13　Collinses call their home "The Do It Homestead" because Charlie and Fran
14　understood that if they wanted to get anything done, they had to "DO IT"
15　themselves.
16　　Using 24 solar electric panels, the Collinses produce enough electricity to
17　meet their needs for three to five days with no sunlight. They run lights, a solar
18　refrigerator/freezer, and other household appliances, such as a dishwasher,
19　washing machine, and vacuum cleaner.

20	Charlie's dream is to help others become as self-reliant as he and his wife
21	are on their Utah homestead. He is the author of "Ask Mr. Solar," a popular
22	newspaper column that answers people's questions about solar energy. Charlie
23	and Fran Collins also teach a college course about solar energy through the
24	Internet. For people who are interested in alternative energy, the Collinses are
25	experienced sources of information. The knowledge they have can be invaluable
26	to anyone who dreams of providing power to their homes without having to pay
27	monthly electric bills.

Questions for Another Look

1 How do the Collinses run their home and farm?

_____

2 Why are the Collinses *energy self-sufficient*?
   a. They built their own farm.
   b. They do not rely on electrical companies for power.
   c. They do not use any source of energy.

3 What is one reason why some people want to be energy self-sufficient?

_____

4 Complete the following sentence:

The Collinses call their farm "The Do It Homestead" because _____

_____

5 The Collinses can give you information if you want to become energy self-sufficient because

    a. they have been energy self-sufficient for 21 years

    b. Mr. Collins writes a newspaper column about solar energy

    c. they teach a college course about solar energy

    d. All of the above

Topics for Discussion and Writing

1 Think about people's lives at home, at work, at school, and so on. Describe how oil makes life easier for people.

2 The first reading passage explains the process of changing oil into different products. Think of another process where something is changed into a useful product. Describe the process, for example, of how people change wood into paper.

3 There are many other scientific advances that make life better or easier for us. Work with a classmate and make a list. Then select one and describe it.

4 **Write in your journal.** Imagine there is no more oil in the world. Describe a day in your life without oil.

Follow-Up Activities

J

1 Make a list of the ways you use petrochemical products in your life. When you are finished, compare your list with a classmate's list. What products did you list which were not mentioned in the passage?

MY USES OF PETROLEUM-BASED PRODUCTS					
Housing	Clothing	Personal Uses	Medical Uses	Transportation	Other Uses

2 Refer to the WORLD OIL RESERVES bar graph below. Then answer the questions that follow.

WORLD OIL RESERVES BY REGION

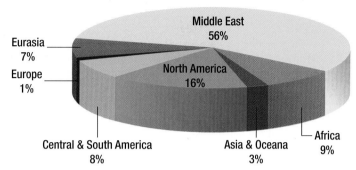

Eurasia 7%

Europe 1%

Middle East 56%

North America 16%

Central & South America 8%

Asia & Oceana 3%

Africa 9%

Data Source: U.S. Energy Information Administration from Oil and Gas Journal (2007).

a. Which region has the largest oil reserves in the world?

_____

b. Which region has the smallest oil reserves in the world?

_____

c. Which region has the second-largest oil reserves in the world?

_____

d. Which one of the following statements is true?

1. The Middle East has smaller oil reserves than all the other countries and areas combined.

2. The Middle East has the same amount of oil reserves as all of the other countries and areas combined.

3. The Middle East has bigger oil reserves than all of the other countries and regions combined.

Word Search

Read the words listed below. Find them in the puzzle and circle them. They may be written in any direction.

adequate	fuel	prescription	refine
aware	heat	process	synthetic
essential	lubricate	realize	transportation

N	O	I	T	A	T	R	O	P	S	N	A	R	T	E
Q	A	Y	Z	H	Q	Z	D	R	T	C	E	J	S	G
W	V	D	B	E	P	F	S	E	A	T	Q	S	L	D
R	M	G	T	L	W	U	Z	S	A	H	E	A	T	C
S	Y	N	T	H	E	T	I	C	E	N	V	A	V	G
R	E	W	A	M	D	U	I	R	T	C	J	W	B	B
E	M	T	G	F	J	R	F	I	H	J	O	A	Q	C
F	Z	G	A	V	B	P	A	P	O	H	C	R	C	H
I	C	I	J	U	D	L	N	T	Q	W	V	E	P	Z
N	G	W	L	E	Q	A	U	I	G	I	S	Y	D	L
E	G	Y	W	A	K	E	H	O	O	P	J	X	A	I
V	X	O	V	Q	E	G	D	N	C	F	N	I	F	M
A	O	A	E	Q	D	R	G	A	A	S	G	J	B	I

Crossword Puzzle

Read the clues on the next two pages. Write the answers in the correct spaces in the puzzle.

Crossword Puzzle Clues

1. Women put _____ on their lips for color.
4. I use a _____ to unlock my door when I come home.
6. Past participle of **run**
7. We need to _____ the moving parts of machines.
11. Nylon is a _____ fiber. Cotton is a natural fiber.
13. When I meet my friend, I _____ hello.
14. _____ are oil-based products.
17. Quiz; exam
18. We use _____ to clean our clothes.
19. John likes tea. I like tea, _____.
20. I will wait _____ you after class.
21. We use _____ to lubricate the moving parts of machines.
23. We use _____ to pave our highways and parking lots. It is black and heavy oil.
24. Food is the most important _____ in our lives, but oil is important, too.
25. The opposite of **lose**
26. We _____ dishes in the kitchen sink.
27. Susan hasn't eaten lunch _____. It's only 10 o'clock.
28. Children love to play with _____.

2. Unclean, dirty
3. He _____ a good math student.
4. _____ is the fuel that airplanes use. They do not use gasoline.
5. Today, many containers are made of _____ instead of glass.
8. The opposite of **girl**
9. I _____ speak two languages.
10. Natural gas is the _____ part of processed oil. Gasoline is heavier.
12. **She,** _____ **, it**
14. Another word for **oil**
15. Oil is a mixture of two elements. Together these two elements are called _____.

16. Automobiles
19. The opposite of **bottom**
20. Cotton and wool are natural _____.
22. Purify; clean
26. You and I

Grammar Cloze Quiz

Read the passage. Complete each blank space with a form of *be* listed below.
You may use the words more than once.

are	is	was	were

In the past, carpets and furniture _____ made from natural materials,
(1)
such as cotton and wood. Today, however, furniture, furniture fabrics,
carpeting, paint, and wallpaper _____ all made from petroleum-based
(2)
synthetics. Our homes _____ heated with oil or natural gas instead of wood.
(3)
These days, some clothing _____ even made from used plastic containers.
(4)
These containers _____ also petrochemical products. The soap we use to
(5)
clean our clothes _____ also a petroleum-based product, but in the past
(6)
soap _____ made from animal fat.
(7)

Petrochemicals have a wide variety of medical uses. Some of the drugs
that our doctors prescribe _____ made of petrochemicals. For example,
(8)
today's aspirin _____ a petrochemical product. Cold medicines that help
(9)
some people breathe more easily _____, too.
(10)

12

How Earthquakes Occur

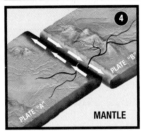

Prereading Preparation

1 Where in the world do earthquakes occur? Do they occur in your country?

2 Look at the illustration. It shows four different ways that earthquakes occur. Read the paragraph below. Using information from both the paragraph and the illustration, fill in the flowchart on page 247.

Track 23

How Earthquakes Occur

1　　The earth's crust, or surface, is made of rock. The crust covers the earth, but it
2　is not in one piece. It is broken into a number of large pieces called plates.
3　These plates are always moving because they lie on top of liquid rock. They slide
4　over the hot, melted rock. The plates move very slowly in different directions.
5　The difference in motion causes the earth's crust to break. This is an earthquake.
6　Earthquakes happen in different ways. In some areas of the earth, the plates
7　move apart. This happens in the middle of the Atlantic Ocean. Earthquakes also
8　take place inside of plates throughout the world. For example, China is being
9　squeezed in two directions, from the east by the Pacific plate and from the south
10　by the India-Australia plate. In other places, plates push directly against each
11　other, and one plate moves downward under the other plate. For instance, this
12　happens off the western coasts of South and Central America and off the coast of
13　Japan. The plates are sliding past one another in other regions of the world, for
14　example, at the San Andreas Fault Zone in California.

FLOWCHART: HOW EARTHQUAKES OCCUR

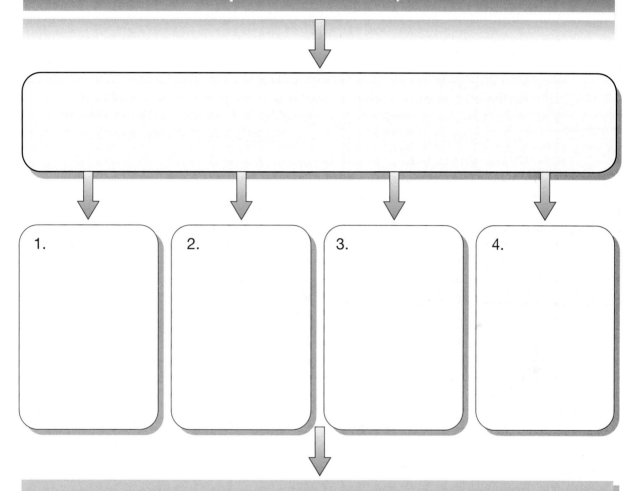

The Earth's plates slide over hot, melted rock.

1.

2.

3.

4.

These are the ways that earthquakes happen.

How Earthquakes Occur

1   Earthquake! People all around the world fear earthquakes because they
2 cause so much destruction and death. Consider the following facts: The
3 Northridge earthquake struck the San Fernando Valley region of Southern
4 California on January 17, 1994. The earthquake caused 61 deaths, over 5,000
5 injuries, and extensive building damage. In fact, some people estimate that
6 the earthquake caused millions of dollars in property damage. The Northridge
7 earthquake ranks as one of the worst natural disasters in U.S. history.
8   On January 17, 1995, the Hyogoken-Nanbu (Kobe) earthquake struck
9 south-central Japan. This earthquake resulted in over 5,500 deaths and many
10 thousands of injuries. The damage costs were estimated at 150 billion
11 U.S. dollars. Although this earthquake was only rated as a moderate-to-large
12 earthquake, it caused so much destruction because it produced a fault break
13 directly through the business area of a city.
14   These statistics are very frightening. Many people wonder if the number of
15 earthquakes is increasing. In reality, the number of earthquakes has actually
16 decreased in recent years. However, because of improved world communication,
17 people receive more news and information than ever before. For example, in the
18 last 20 years, we have been able to locate more earthquakes yearly because there
19 are more seismograph, or earthquake-measuring, stations in the world. These
20 additional stations help seismological centers to locate many small earthquakes
21 that were undetectable years ago.
22   Many scientists are trying to predict earthquakes, but these predictions are
23 very uncertain. Scientists cannot calculate the exact location, time, or intensity
24 of an earthquake. Furthermore, the predicted earthquake may not take place
25 at all. As a result, scientists do not think it is a useful idea to announce that an
26 earthquake will take place on a specific day. Instead, most people are trying
27 to design structures such as buildings, dams, and bridges that can resist
28 earthquakes. People can reduce loss of life, injuries, and property damage by
29 sufficiently preparing themselves, their homes, work places, and communities
30 for a major earthquake. After all, it is possible to survive an earthquake.

Fact-Finding Exercise

Read the passage once. Then read the following statements. Check whether they are True or False. If a statement is false, rewrite it so that it is true. Then go back to the passage and find the line that supports your answer.

1 _____ True _____ False   The earthquake damage in Kobe was more costly than the earthquake damage in Northridge.

_____

2 _____ True _____ False   More people were killed in the earthquake in Northridge than were killed in the earthquake in Kobe.

_____

3 _____ True _____ False   In recent years, the number of earthquakes has increased.

_____

4 _____ True _____ False   There are more seismological centers in the world today than there were in the past.

_____

5 _____ True _____ False   Scientists cannot predict when an earthquake will occur.

_____

6 _____ True _____ False   We cannot protect ourselves from earthquakes.

_____

Skimming and Scanning Exercise

PART 1

Skim through the passage. Then read the following statements. Choose the one that is the correct main idea of the reading.

a. Earthquakes, which occur all over the world, cause death, injuries, and destruction, and are very difficult to predict.
b. Earthquakes occur all over the world, but we can protect ourselves if we are prepared.
c. There are many seismological centers all over the world that can tell us when an earthquake occurs.

PART 2

Scan the passage. Work with a partner to fill in the chart with information from the reading.

EARTHQUAKES			
Place	Number of Injuries	Number of Deaths	Cost of Damage
Northridge			
Kobe			
Ways to reduce the possibility of earthquake damage			

Reading Analysis

Read each question carefully. Either circle the letter or the number of the correct answer, or write your answer in the space provided.

1 People all around the world fear earthquakes because they cause so much destruction and death. **Consider the following facts:** The Northridge earthquake struck the San Fernando Valley region of Southern California on January 17, 1994. The earthquake caused 61 deaths, **over 5,000 injuries,** and extensive building damage. **In fact,** some people estimate that the earthquake caused millions of dollars in property damage. The Northridge earthquake ranks as **one of the worst natural disasters in U.S. history.**

a. **Consider the following facts** means
   1. think about this information
   2. remember this information
   3. be afraid of this information

b. **over 5,000 injuries** means
   1. exactly 5,000 people were hurt
   2. more than 5,000 people were hurt
   3. fewer than 5,000 people were hurt

c. What information follows **in fact?**
   1. Different information that introduces a new idea
   2. Additional information that gives more details about the previous sentence
   3. True information that everyone believes

d. How does the Northridge earthquake rank as a U.S. natural disaster?
   1. Very bad, but not the worst
   2. The worst

e. Which of the following can also be natural disasters?
   1. Car accidents
   2. Hurricanes
   3. Floods
   4. House fires
   5. Tornadoes
   6. Forest fires
   7. Murders

2 On January 17, 1995, the Hyogoken-Nanbu (Kobe) earthquake struck south-central Japan. This earthquake resulted in over 5,500 deaths and many thousands of injuries. **The damage costs were estimated at 150 billion U.S. dollars.**

The estimated damage was

a. a little less than $150 billion
b. approximately $150 billion
c. more than $150 billion

3 **These statistics are very frightening.** Many people wonder if the number of earthquakes is actually increasing. **In reality,** the number of earthquakes has actually decreased in recent years.

a. What are **these statistics?**

1. The number of earthquakes that happen every year in California and Japan
2. The number of people who died in earthquakes in the last few years in California and Japan
3. The number of deaths and injuries, and the amount of destruction caused by the earthquakes in Kobe and California

b. What information follows **in reality?**

1. True information which shows that the information in the previous sentence was correct
2. True information which shows that the information in the previous sentence is incorrect
3. Additional information that gives more details about the previous sentence

4 In the last 20 years, we have been able to locate more earthquakes yearly because there are more **seismographic, or earthquake-measuring, stations** in the world. These additional stations help seismological centers to locate many small earthquakes which were **undetectable** years ago.

a. What does a **seismographic measuring station** do?

_____

b. **Undetectable** means

1. unnoticeable
2. lost
3. unimportant

5 Many scientists are trying to predict earthquakes, but these predictions are very uncertain. Scientists cannot **calculate** the exact location, time, or intensity of an earthquake. **Furthermore,** the **predicted** earthquake may not take place at all.

a. **Predict** means
   1. stop something from happening
   2. tell something will happen before it happens
   3. understand something by reading about it

b. **Calculate** means
   1. tell everyone
   2. see
   3. figure out

c. What information comes after **furthermore?**
   1. More information about the same subject
   2. The same information in different words
   3. The result of the information before furthermore

6 Many scientists are trying to predict earthquakes, but these predictions are very uncertain. The predicted earthquake may not take place at all. **As a result,** they do not think it is a useful idea to announce that an earthquake will take place on a specific day.

a. Why don't scientists think it is a useful idea to announce that an earthquake will take place?
   1. Because they don't want people to protect themselves
   2. Because they are not sure what time the earthquake will occur
   3. Because the predicted earthquake might not take place at all

b. Finish the following sentence with the correct selection.

   Elizabeth read several interesting books about earthquakes.
   As a result,
   1. she became a better reader
   2. she decided to live in California
   3. she learned many new facts about earthquakes

c. **As a result** means
   1. moreover
   2. consequently
   3. however

7 Scientists do not think it is a useful idea to announce that an earthquake will take place on a specific day. **Instead,** more people are trying to design structures such as buildings, dams, and bridges that can **resist** earthquakes.

a. **Instead** introduces

1. an idea that is similar to the previous idea
2. an idea that gives more details about the previous idea
3. an idea that takes the place of the previous idea

b. A building that can **resist** an earthquake

1. will fall down
2. will not fall down

D Dictionary Skills

Read the dictionary entry for each word and think about the context of the sentence. Write the number of the appropriate definition on the line next to the word. In addition, circle *noun, verb,* or *adjective* where indicated. Then choose the sentence with the correct answer.

1

> **surface** *n.* **1** the outside layer of an object: *Rocks found on the beach usually have a smooth surface.* **2** the flat top level of s.t.: *the surface of a table (a pond, a mirror)* **3** outward appearance: *On the surface, that looks like a good car, but the engine is bad.* **4** **to skim the surface:** to treat superficially: *The solution that you propose only skims the surface of the problem.*
>
> —*v.* **-faced, -facing, -faces** **1** [I] to rise to the surface: *We saw two whales surface and then dive back into the ocean.* **2** [I] to appear: *That problem surfaced when our mechanic examined the car.* **3** [T] to cover a road with asphalt or paving material: *They surfaced the new road last week.*

To understand what causes earthquakes, we need to understand the nature of the earth and the changes that are slowly taking place in the earth's **surface,** or crust, which is made of rock.

a. **surface:** _____ (noun / verb / adjective)

b. 1. We need to understand the nature of the earth and the changes that are slowly taking place in the outside layer of the earth.
   2. We need to understand the nature of the earth and the changes that are slowly taking place in the flat top level of the earth.
   3. We need to understand the nature of the earth and the changes that are slowly taking place in the outward appearance of the earth.

2 **strike** *v.* struck, struck or stricken **1** [I; T] *(syns.)* to punch, slap ‖ pound, hit: *She* **struck** *her brother and gave him a bloody nose. She* **punched** *her brother.* ‖ *The hammer* **struck** *the nail. The hammer* **pounded** *the nail.*
2 [I; T] *(syns.)* to smash into s.t., collide with s.t.: *The car rolled down the hill and* **struck** *a tree. The car rolled down the hill and* **smashed into** *a tree (or)* **collided with** *a tree.* **3** [I; T] *(syn.)* to attack: *The army* **struck** *by surprise at night. The army* **attacked** *by surprise at night.* **4** [I; T] *(syns.)* to come to one (s.o.'s mind suddenly), dawn on s.o.: *A good idea* **struck** *me as I was reading the newspaper. A good idea* **came to me** *(or)* **dawned on me** *as I was reading the newspaper.* **5** [I; T] *(syns.)* to impress, affect s.o.: *The power of her words* **struck** *me as beautiful. The power of her words* **impressed** *me as beautiful.* **6** [I; T] *(syns.)* to discover, come upon s.t.: *The workers* **will strike** *oil (gold, silver, diamonds), if they dig deep enough. The workers* **will discover** *oil etc. (or) come upon oil (gold, silver, diamonds) if they dig deep enough.* **7** [T] *(syns.)* to erase, eliminate: **Strike the second paragraph, but keep the first and third ones. Erase (or) eliminate the second paragraph, but keep the first and third ones.** **8** [I] *(syn.)* to walk out, as in to go on strike: *The bus drivers are* **striking** *until the owners give them more vacation time. The bus drivers are* **walking out** *(or)* **going on strike** *until the owners give them more vacation time.* **9** [T] *(syn.)* to light s.t. (a fire): *I* **lit** *a match to light my cigarette.* **10** [I; T] *(syns.)* to play ‖ sound s.t.: *He* **struck** *C-sharp on the piano. He* **played** *C-sharp on the piano.* ‖ *The clock* **struck** *midnight. The clock* **sounded** *midnight.*

The Northridge earthquake **struck** the San Fernando Valley region of Southern California on January 17, 1994.

a. strike: _____ (noun / verb / adjective)

b. 1. The Northridge earthquake appeared suddenly in the San Fernando Valley region of Southern California on January 17, 1994.
   2. The Northridge earthquake ran into the San Fernando Valley region of Southern California on January 17, 1994.
   3. The Northridge earthquake hit the San Fernando Valley region of Southern California on January 17, 1994.

3 **fault** *n.* **1** an imperfection, flaw: *There is a fault in the computer system.* **2** a weak point in s.o.'s character, shortcoming, foible: *He has some faults, such as sometimes talking too much.* **3** blame, responsibility (for a mistake): *Nobody knew who was at fault for the train accident.* **4** a large crack in the surface of the earth: *The San Andreas fault lies near San Francisco, where the fault line runs north and south.* **5** **to a fault**: more than is necessary: *That man is careful in his business dealings to a fault.* **6** **to find fault with**: to criticize usu. too often, *(syn.)* to carp about: *He complained that his boss was always finding fault with his work.*

The Kobe earthquake caused so much destruction because it produced a **fault** break directly through the business area of a city.

a. **fault:** _____ (noun / verb / adjective)

b. 1. The Kobe earthquake caused so much destruction because it produced an imperfection directly through the business area of a city.

2. The Kobe earthquake is blamed for so much destruction because it produced a break directly through the business area of a city.

3. The Kobe earthquake caused so much destruction because it produced a large crack in the earth's surface directly through the business area of a city.

4 **survive** *v.* [I; T] **-vived, -viving, -vives** **1** to continue to live or exist, esp. for a long time or under hard conditions: *This tree has survived for many years.* **2** to outlast adversity or a threat to existence: *She was lucky to survive the plane crash.*

People can reduce loss of life, injuries, and property damage by sufficiently preparing themselves, their homes, work places, and communities for a major earthquake. After all, it is possible to **survive** an earthquake.

a. **survive:** _____ (noun / verb / adjective)

b. 1. After all, it is possible to prepare for and endure an earthquake.

2. After all, it is possible to prepare for and outlast an earthquake.

3. After all, it is possible to threaten an earthquake.

E Word Forms

In English, some verbs become nouns by adding the suffix *-ment,* for example, *improve (v.), improvement (n.).* Complete each sentence with the correct form of the word on the left. **Write all the verbs in the simple present tense. They may be affirmative or negative. The nouns may be singular or plural.**

move *(v.)*

movement *(n.)*

1. The continents _____ on plates on the earth's crust. We don't notice the _____ because it is very slow.

place *(v.)*

placement *(n.)*

2. Schools usually _____ new students into different English classes depending on their English abilities. The students' _____ depend on the scores they get on an English test.

announce *(v.)*

announcement *(n.)*

3. Television stations interrupt programs to make important _____ as soon as they receive the news. However, the stations generally _____ small news items until the regular news programs.

measure *(v.)*

measurement *(n.)*

4. Many scientists _____ the intensity of an earthquake with a Richter scale. The Richter scale's _____ range from 1 to 10, where 10 is the most intense.

require *(v.)*

requirement *(n.)*

5. Most American colleges have an English _____ for foreign students. For instance, many colleges generally _____ a TOEFL score of 500 or higher.

In English, the noun form and the verb form of some words are the same, for example, *cover (v.)*, *cover (n.)*. Complete each sentence with the correct form of the word on the left. Circle *(v.)* if you are using the verb or *(n.)* if you are using the noun form of each word. **Write all the verbs in the simple present tense. They may be affirmative or negative. The nouns may be singular or plural.**

fear

1　Tom has a terrible ＿＿＿＿＿＿ of airplanes. Tom
　　　　　　　　　　　　(v., n.)

＿＿＿＿＿＿ airplanes so much that he never even goes
(v., n.)

to airports.

change

2　People need to make many ＿＿＿＿＿＿ when they
　　　　　　　　　　　　　　　　(v., n.)

move to another country. However, they ＿＿＿＿＿＿
　　　　　　　　　　　　　　　　　　　　　(v., n.)

everything in their lives!

break

3　The movement of the earth ＿＿＿＿＿＿ many man-made
　　　　　　　　　　　　　　　　　(v., n.)

objects that are underground, such as telephone

and power lines, and gas and water pipelines. Any

＿＿＿＿＿＿ in a gas line can cause dangerous fires
(v., n.)

wherever an earthquake occurs.

damage

4　Earthquakes of high intensity cause a lot of ＿＿＿＿＿＿
　　　　　　　　　　　　　　　　　　　　　　　(v., n.)

to buildings, roads, and bridges. Earthquakes also

＿＿＿＿＿＿ homes, dams, and gas and water pipelines.
(v., n.)

design

5 Eve has a book full of her own _____ for women's
(v., n.)

clothes. However, she is only interested in formal clothes.

She _____ sports or casual clothes.
(v., n.)

Word Partnership	Use *requirement* with:
adj.	**legal** requirement, **minimum** requirement
v.	**meet a** requirement

Vocabulary in Context

as a result	in reality	requirement *(n.)*	surface *(n.)*
calculate *(v.)*	predict *(v.)*	statistics *(n.)*	survive *(v.)*

Read the following sentences. Complete each blank space with the correct word or phrase from the list above. Use each word or phrase only once.

1 Isabella thought that John didn't like her. _____, John liked her a lot, but he didn't speak to her because he was very shy.

2 Good eyesight is a _____ for an airline pilot. You need it in order to fly a plane.

3 A human being cannot _____ without water for more than a week.

4 Can you help me _____ how many miles per gallon I will get from my car? I want to know how much gas I will need for my trip.

5 No one knows exactly when an earthquake will occur. No one can _____ when a volcano will erupt, either.

6 The _____ of the moon has no water. However, there may be frozen water underneath.

7 According to _____, more than 30,000 earthquakes occurred in 2008. This number is higher than the number of earthquakes in 2007.

8 Greg forgot his house keys. _____, he couldn't get into his home until his father returned from work.

G

Think About It

Read the following questions and think about the answers. Write your answer below each question. Then compare your answers with those of your classmates.

1 Some areas of the earth experience earthquakes often, especially places such as California and Japan. Why do people continue to live where earthquakes are likely to take place?

_____

_____

_____

2 Scientists do not think it is a good idea to announce an earthquake because it may not actually take place. Do you agree with the scientists? Explain your answer.

_____

_____

_____

3 What other natural disasters do people need to prepare themselves for? How can they prepare for these disasters?

_____

_____

_____

Another Look

Read the earthquake survivor's story. Then answer the questions that follow.

A Survivor's Story

1   My name is Keiko Tanaka, and I live in Kobe, Japan. Because I was born and
2 raised in Japan, I have experienced many earthquakes. By far the most powerful
3 and frightening earthquake I have ever lived through was the one that struck my
4 city on January 17, 1995.
5   My son's family and I live in a small house in Kobe. When the earthquake
6 began, it was only 5:46 A.M., and we were all sleeping. I was thrown from my
7 bed onto the carpet. I wanted to get to my son and his wife, but I couldn't—the
8 amount of movement in our home was incredible. The door near where I was
9 standing was swinging back and forth. I listened helplessly while just about
10 everything standing in our home fell over. Loose objects were tossed across
11 rooms while the shaking continued. The noise was incredibly loud. When the
12 earthquake finally stopped, I hurried to my son's room, where he, his wife Mika,
13 and their children had been sleeping. Then we looked around our home. It had
14 been heavily damaged. All the windows were broken, and the roof had fallen in.
15 In the kitchen, most of the dishes lay in small pieces all across the kitchen floor.
16 Outside, we saw that our neighbors' houses had fallen down, too. People were
17 standing near their homes, and everyone looked shocked and frightened.
18   Although we were all safe and no one had been hurt, we were still very
19 affected by a terrible fear. In addition, we did not have electrical power or water
20 for days. Overall, it was a terrifying experience, and we worry that it may
21 happen again. In the meantime, we are all beginning to try to rebuild our homes
22 and our lives. We love our beautiful city of Kobe and do not want to leave it.

Questions for Another Look

1 The writer says that **". . . because I was born and raised in Japan, I have experienced a lot of earthquakes."** This sentence tells us that

    a. the writer speaks Japanese
    b. Japan has a lot of earthquakes
    c. earthquakes are very frightening

2 Why was the noise **incredibly loud** during the earthquake?

_____

_____

3 What kind of damage did the Tanaka home have after the earthquake?

_____

_____

4 Do you think the Tanaka family will continue to live in Kobe? Why or why not?

_____

_____

I   Topics for Discussion and Writing

1 If you know someone who experienced an earthquake, interview that person. Then write a composition describing the person's experience.

2 Form a team of three. Imagine that an earthquake took place an hour ago. Your team must organize a rescue in your school building. Decide what you have to do. List these actions in their order of importance. Assign responsibilities to each member of the team. Have each team member write a composition describing his or her plan of action.

3 Imagine that you are a teacher. Prepare a set of instructions for your students. Tell them what to do if an earthquake occurs.

4 **Write in your journal.** Imagine that an earthquake took place where you live. Describe the experience. What happened immediately before the earthquake? What happened during the earthquake? What happened after the earthquake? What did you think about? How did you feel?

J Follow-Up Activities

1 A seismograph is an instrument that scientists use to locate and record earthquakes. Scientists measure the energy, or intensity, of earthquakes with a Richter scale. The Richter scale measures the intensity, or strength, of earthquakes on a scale of 1 to 10. Look at the map below and read the list of earthquakes around the world on the next page. Write the number next to the star that indicates the location of each earthquake.

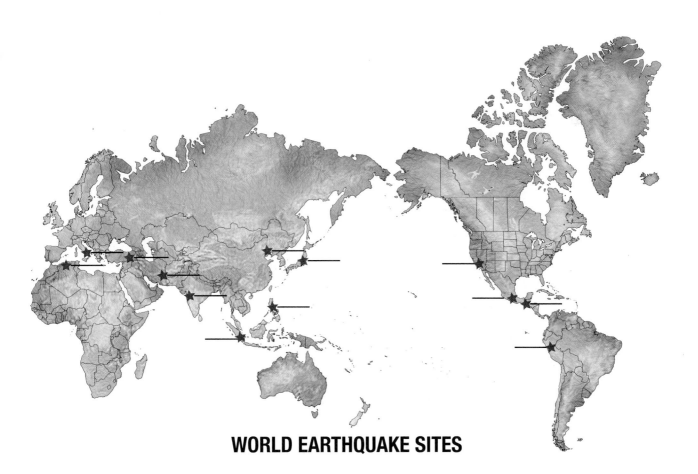

WORLD EARTHQUAKE SITES

2 Look at the chart below and answer the questions that follow.

DEADLY EARTHQUAKES AROUND THE WORLD			
Date	Location	Intensity on Richter Scale	Number of Deaths
1. 2/76	Guatemala	7.5	23,000
2. 8/76	The Philippines	8.0	6,500
3. 9/85	Mexico City	8.1	9,000
4. 3/92	Eastern Turkey	6.2	4,000
5. 1/94	Northridge, California	6.8	61
6. 1/95	Kobe, Japan	7.2	5,500
7. 1/01	Gujarat, India	7.6	20,000
8. 5/03	Northern Algeria	6.8	2,300
9. 12/03	Southeastern Iran	6.6	13,000
10. 12/04	Sumatra-Andaman Islands	9.1	228,000
11. 8/07	Near Coast of Peru	8.0	500
12. 5/08	Eastern Sichuan, China	7.9	88,000
13. 4/09	Central Italy	6.3	300

a. Where was the earthquake with the highest intensity on the Richter scale?

_____

b. Where were the most people killed in an earthquake?

_____

c. Why were so many people killed there? What do you think?

_____

d. In some places, earthquakes kill fewer than 1,000 people, while in other places many thousands of people die. What might be some reasons why more people are killed in some places than in others? What do you think?

_____

_____

3 a. Read the following checklist for home safety during an earthquake.

1. Make sure that hanging lights are not above beds.
2. Make sure that beds are not right below heavy mirrors.
3. Make sure that beds are not right below framed pictures.
4. Make sure that beds are not right below shelves with lots of objects that can fall.
5. Make sure that beds are not next to large windows.
6. Take all heavy objects off high shelves.
7. Take all breakable objects off high shelves.
8. Make sure that heavy mirrors are well fastened to walls.
9. Make sure that heavy pictures are well fastened to walls.
10. Make sure that air conditioners are well supported in windows.

b. Look at the following bedroom. Refer to the checklist. In pairs or small groups, decide how to make the bedroom safer in the event of an earthquake. When you are finished, compare your safer bedroom with another group's bedroom.

4 It is important to know what to do during an earthquake. Read the following list. In pairs, decide what to do and what not to do during an earthquake. When you finish, compare your list with another pair of students. Be prepared to give reasons for your decisions.

_____ Yes _____ No   **a.** Stay calm and don't do anything to upset other people.

_____ Yes _____ No   **b.** Run to other rooms and shout, "Earthquake! Earthquake!"

_____ Yes _____ No   **c.** If you are indoors, get under a desk or a table, if possible.

_____ Yes _____ No   **d.** If you are in a high building, take the elevator to the first floor.

_____ Yes _____ No   **e.** If you are in a building, do not run outside. Falling objects are a danger.

_____ Yes _____ No   **f.** If you are outside near a building, stand in a doorway.

_____ Yes _____ No   **g.** If you are outside, but not near a building, try to get into an open area away from buildings and power lines.

_____ Yes _____ No   **h.** If you are in a car, continue driving to get as far away from the earthquake as possible.

_____ Yes _____ No   **i.** If the electrical power lines and gas lines break, use matches and candles for light.

_____ Yes _____ No   **j.** If you are in an empty room with no desk or table, stand in a doorway.

UNIT 6   THE EARTH'S RESOURCES AND DANGERS

Word Search

Read the words listed below. Find them in the puzzle and circle them. They may be written in any direction.

actual	earthquake	locate	predict
consider	furthermore	natural	resist
design	increase	occur	statistics

```
E  R  O  M  R  E  H  T  R  U  F  Z  S  C  L
S  K  Q  R  S  I  H  L  S  D  W  V  X  L  D
A  L  A  R  U  T  A  N  O  S  C  W  N  A  F
E  U  C  U  X  L  S  O  C  C  U  R  G  P  S
R  N  T  R  Q  R  T  O  E  O  A  G  I  W  O
C  L  U  I  K  H  A  N  K  N  B  T  S  H  Y
N  G  A  E  G  D  T  P  T  S  I  S  E  R  E
I  G  L  Z  F  M  I  R  D  I  Z  C  D  H  K
E  E  H  C  C  H  S  E  A  D  W  W  R  Y  Y
F  A  D  L  A  Z  T  D  I  E  Z  X  K  T  C
C  M  Z  L  L  V  I  I  F  R  V  O  E  W  N
J  Y  V  K  Z  L  C  C  K  K  S  P  X  N  R
O  G  U  V  S  U  S  T  C  Q  X  K  E  S  A
```

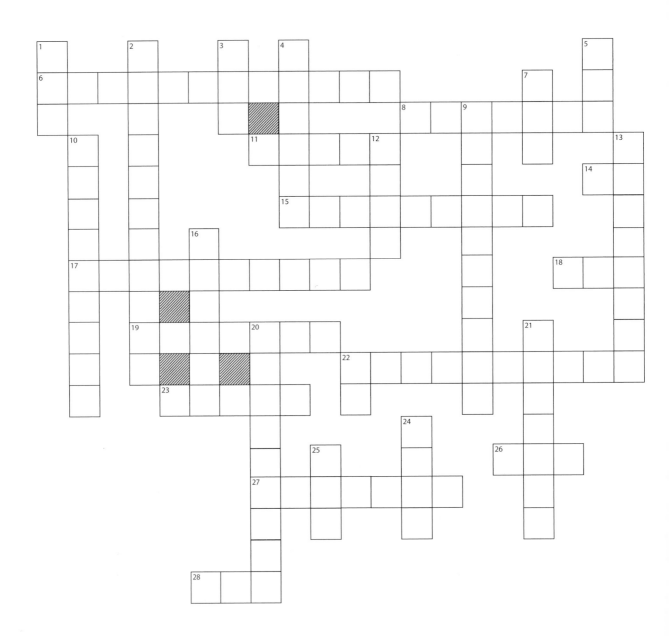

Crossword Puzzle

Read the clues on the next two pages. Write the answers in the correct spaces in the puzzle.

Crossword Puzzle Clues

6. Some small earthquakes are _____ or unnoticeable.
8. I wanted coffee, but I drank tea _____.
11. The Tangshan earthquake _____ as the most deadly earthquake of all time.
14. We have class _____ Wednesday.
15. The Kobe earthquake cost an _____ $150 billion.
17. An _____ happens when the earth moves and the ground breaks up.
18. I have a birthday present _____ you.
19. Scientists cannot _____ the weather or earthquakes.
22. Dams, buildings, and bridges are _____.
23. Tell; say
26. Mark _____ swim very well.
27. Many people _____ earthquakes. Others do not; they are killed.
28. Scientists know _____ and how earthquakes occur. They don't know when.

1. The _____ is the star closest to the Earth.
2. A _____ is a machine for detecting earthquakes.
3. When an earthquake takes place, people need to _____ quickly to protect themselves.
4. Earthquakes cause a lot of _____ to buildings and roads.
5. The opposite of **subtract**
7. The opposite of **no**
9. The records of earthquake damage, deaths, and injuries are very frightening _____.
10. The number of earthquakes did not increase. The number _____ .
12. The past tense of **slide**
13. Earthquakes kill some people, and cause _____ to other people.
16. The _____ of earthquakes is very high in some areas of the world.

20. The _____, or severity, of an earthquake is measured on a Richter scale.
21. The _____ of the Earth is called the crust.
22. Ann was tired, _____ she went to sleep.
24. I _____ a book about earthquakes. I bought it last week.
25. Scientists _____ trying to learn more about earthquakes.

M Grammar Cloze Quiz

Read the passage below. Complete each blank space with an article.

a	an	the

_____ earth's crust is broken into _____ number of large pieces called
(1)   (2)

plates. _____ continents ride on top of _____ plates, and move with them.
(3)   (4)

_____ plates move very slowly, usually at _____ rate of about _____ inch
(5)   (6)   (7)

per year.

_____ plates move in different directions. _____ difference in motion
(8)   (9)

causes the rocks to break. This is _____ earthquake. _____ earthquake
(10)   (11)

happens in different ways. In some areas of _____ earth, _____ plates move
(12)   (13)

apart. This happens in _____ middle of _____ Atlantic Ocean. _____ plates
(14)   (15)   (16)

are sliding past one another in other regions of _____ world, for example,
(17)

at _____ San Andreas fault zone in California. In other places, plates push
(18)

directly against each other, and one plate moves downward under another

plate. For example, _____ plate is moving under another one off _____
(19)   (20)

western coasts of South and Central America and off the coasts of Japan.

1. The earth produces oil, which is very useful. The earth also creates earthquakes, which are very destructive. Work with a classmate. Make a list of other things that the earth produces which are very useful. Then make a list of other things that the earth produces which are destructive. Explain your choices.

_____

_____

_____

_____

_____

2. Look over your list from #1. Choose one thing that the earth produces which is useful. Then choose one of the things that the earth produces which is destructive. Describe them in more detail.

_____

_____

_____

_____

_____

INDEX OF KEY WORDS AND PHRASES

Words in blue are on the Academic Word List (AWL), Coxhead (2000). The AWL is a list of the 570 highest-frequency academic word families that regularly appear in academic texts. The list was compiled by researcher Averil Coxhead from a corpus of 3.5 million words.

A

ability, 89, 101
according to, 189
acetaminophen, 224
across, 3, 261
actually, 132, 152, 237, 248
addition, 89, 110, 143, 189, 248, 261
adequate, 225
adopt, 63, 77
adoptees, 63, 64
adoption, 63, 78
adoptive, 64, 77
advice, 143, 165
advise, 143, 152
after all, 152, 248
agency, 78
airfare, 22
Alamo, 12
all the same, 177
aloud, 132
alternative, 238
although, 78, 90, 101, 151, 225, 248, 261
amazed, 89, 178
ancient, 223
announced, 90, 177, 248
answer, 42, 165, 238
apparent, 212
appliances, 237
as a matter of fact, 63
as a result of, 152
as a result, 132, 248
asphalt, 224, 225
assembling, 89
assistance, 143
attendance, 101
award, 178, 189, 190, 199, 212
aware, 212

B

backwards, 109
bacteria, 223
biological, 41, 62, 63
birth mother, 64
birth parents, 63, 64
birthplace, 3
blood pressure, 132
bond, 55
bored, 165
bumpers, 224

C

calculate, 248
calmer, 131
calming, 132
cancer, 152
candidate, 190
carbon, 223
cause, 199, 246, 248
cellist, 89
characteristics, 41
classmate, 3
close, 41, 77, 199
coincidence, 41
communicate, 42, 78
communication, 78, 248
community, 31, 248
concentrate, 41
concert, 89
conduct, 89
confidential, 63
confuse, 41, 151
consequently, 152
construct, 22, 177
control, 101, 109
convenience, 237
counselor, 143
couple, 63
crew, 12
crude, 224, 225
crust, 246
curb, 110
curious, 41

D

Dacron, 224
dairy, 151, 152
damage, 248, 261
dams, 177
dangerous, 89, 177, 199
deliver, 109
design, 89, 248
destruction, 248
develop, 152
device, 110, 121
diaper, 54
diet, 151, 152
dieting, 165
direction, 109, 246
disaster, 248

discovered, 41, 198
discovery, 55, 190, 199
discuss, 110, 198
disturbed, 177
dormitories, 22
dream, 3, 237, 238
dynamite, 177

E

earthquake, 246, 247, 248, 261
effective, 132
electricity, 109, 237, 238, 261
elements, 199, 223
encourage, 110, 120, 121
environment, 41, 42, 109, 121, 132, 237
environmental, 237
environmentally friendly, 237
equipment, 54
equipped, 89
ESP, 41
essential, 224, 225
establish, 178, 189, 190
estimate, 248
even though, 55, 64
eventually, 223
experiences, 3, 31, 41, 54, 238, 261
explosive, 177
exposure, 199, 212
extensive, 248

F

fabrics, 224
factories, 89
fatigue, 199
fault, 246, 248
for example, 22, 31, 41, 42, 109, 120, 121, 131, 132, 152, 224, 246, 248
for instance, 22, 41, 132, 152, 224, 246
former, 21, 89
fortune, 177, 178, 189
forwards, 109
friendliness, 41
furnace, 224, 225
furthermore, 248

G

grains, 151, 152
grease, 224
guide, 151

H

harmful, 151
healthy, 131, 151, 152
heart disease, 132, 152
high-fat, 152
honor, 178
however, 31, 55, 63, 89, 101, 143, 151, 177, 199, 212, 224, 237, 248
humanity, 21
hydrocarbons, 223
hydrogen, 223

I

identical, 41, 42
immigrant, 31
impure, 224
in addition, 89, 143, 261
in addition to, 110, 189
in any case, 63
in contrast, 152
in fact, 31, 41, 63, 78, 89, 131, 132, 152, 177, 189, 198, 199, 224, 248
in order to, 31, 151, 177, 199
in other words, 224
in reality, 248
in spite of, 198
in the past, 224
incredibly, 261
inexpensive, 198
influences, 41
inherited, 41
injuries, 248
instead, 3, 131, 143, 165, 166, 224, 248
intensity, 248
Internet, 12, 238
interviewed, 3
invented, 109, 110, 120, 121, 177
invention, 109, 110, 120, 121
isolated, 199

J

journal, 3
journey, 178
jury, 190

K

kindergarten, 55, 78

L

lap, 131
Last Will and Testament, 178
leukemia, 212
limit, 225
location, 22, 248
lonely, 131
lubricate, 224, 225

M

machines, 89, 110, 224, 237
medical, 22, 64, 110, 198, 224
medicine, 110, 178, 189, 198, 224
mixed feelings, 64
mixture, 78
motion, 246

N

nationality, 177, 178
naturally, 41, 64
not only . . . but also, 89
not to mention, 54
nutrition, 166
nylon, 224

O

on the other hand, 152
once, 55, 198
orchestra, 89
organic, 223
organization, 21, 22, 31, 132
Orlon, 224
orphanage, 77
outstanding, 189, 190
overall, 261
owner, 132, 189

P

packaging, 89
pain, 41, 42, 132, 224
parenthood, 54
patient, 110, 132
performed, 89
perhaps, 42
perseverance, 199
personality, 41
pet, 131, 132
petrochemicals, 224
petroleum, 223, 224, 225
plate, 246
pollution, 109
polonium, 199
polyester, 224
popular, 31, 90, 152, 177, 238
portable, 54
power, 131, 238, 261
powerful, 132, 177, 261
predict, 248
prediction, 248
pregnant, 54
prescribe, 224
pressure, 132, 223
prize, 21, 120, 178, 189, 190, 198, 199, 212
protect, 63
publish, 3

R

race, 63
radiation, 199, 212
radioactivity, 199, 212
radium, 199
Rayon, 224
real estate, 3
recognize, 89
refine, 224
relaxed, 131, 143
relieve, 143, 224
reliever, 224
remain, 223, 225
replace, 90, 101
reports, 3, 178
research, 22, 42, 152, 190, 198, 199
resource, 224
robot, 89, 90, 101

S

scared, 64, 101
scientific, 198
scientists, 22, 41, 42, 101, 190, 198, 248
scooter, 109
sealed, 63
sedimentary, 223
Segway, 109, 110
seismograph, 248
seismological, 248
self-confidence, 132
self-sacrifice, 199
self-sufficient, 237
senior citizen, 31, 90
separated, 41
shaped, 89
shyness, 41
sibling, 55
similar, 41
similarity, 41
single, 90
skill, 21, 22, 31, 132
solar energy, 237, 238
solution, 22
station, 12, 248
statistics, 248
still, 31, 41, 42, 55, 261
straight ahead, 109
stress, 131, 143, 165
substance, 224
such as, 22, 41, 89, 109, 121, 152, 198, 224, 237, 248
support, 198
surface, 246
surroundings, 41
survive, 248, 261
synthetic, 224

T

team, 190
technology, 12, 121
Texas, 12
therapy, 131, 132
though, 41, 55, 64
tragic, 199
triplet, 54, 55
twins, 41, 42

U

uncertain, 42, 248
undetectable, 248
unfortunately, 152, 198, 212
uninteresting, 89

unusual, 3, 41, 101
upset, 177
USDA, 151
useful, 90, 109, 110, 120, 121, 143, 151, 224, 248

V

vacation, 21, 22
vacuum, 90, 237
valuable, 224
van, 3
veterinarian, 131
vinyl, 224
violence, 177
volunteer, 21, 22, 21, 132

W

weapons, 177
wheelchair, 110
will, 22, 42, 55, 64, 77, 78, 90, 101, 109, 121, 143, 152, 178, 115, 248
world, 22, 64, 151, 152, 177, 178, 212, 224, 225, 246, 248
worry, 64, 143, 261

X

X ray, 212

SKILLS INDEX

GRAMMAR AND USAGE

Grammar cloze quizzes, 19, 36–37, 61, 86, 107, 127, 149, 174, 196, 219, 245, 270

Word forms

Adjectives that become nouns by adding -*ness*, 50, 209

Identical noun and verb forms, 8, 51–52, 73–74, 97–98, 115–116, 139–140, 162–163, 234–235, 258–259

Nouns that become adjectives by adding -*ful*, 138

Nouns that become verbs by adding -*ment*, 161

Verbs that become nouns by adding -*ance* or -*ence*, 208

Verbs that become nouns by adding -*ion*, 74–75, 116–117

Verbs that become nouns by adding -*ion* or -*ation*, 185

Verbs that become nouns by adding -*ment*, 96, 186, 257

Verbs that become nouns by adding -*tion*, 27–28, 233

Word partnerships, 9, 28, 52, 75, 98, 117, 140, 163, 186, 209, 235, 259

INTERNET

Searching, 192

LISTENING/SPEAKING

Describing, 40, 62, 170

Discussion, 174, 192, 265, 266

Topics, 14, 33, 37, 57, 79–80, 102, 122, 144, 167, 191, 214, 239, 262–263

Explanations, 170, 171

Group activities, 15, 20, 102, 130, 131, 144, 170, 174, 192, 262, 265, 266

Instructing, 262

Interviewing, 57, 262

Ordering in restaurants, 170

Partner activities, 15, 171, 174, 265, 266

Reporting, 15, 20, 82, 123, 151

Surveying, 131

READING

Checklists, 265

Comprehension

Categorization, 13, 56

Charts, 80–81

Crossword puzzles, 17–18, 35–36, 59–60, 84–85, 105–106, 125–126, 147–148, 172–173, 194–195, 217–218, 243–245, 268–270

Dictionary skills, 7–8, 26–27, 48–49, 72–73, 95, 114–115, 137, 160, 183–184, 206–207, 231–232, 254–256

Follow-up activities, 14, 33, 57, 80–82, 145, 168–171, 191–192, 215, 240

Grammar cloze quizzes, 174

Group activities, 77

Lists, 15

Maps, 12, 15

Multiple-choice questions, 5, 6–7, 13, 24, 25–26, 32, 40, 43, 44–47, 66, 67–71, 79, 89, 91, 92–94, 112, 113–114, 134–136, 144, 154, 156, 157, 158–159, 176, 179, 180–182, 197–198, 201, 202–203, 204–205, 213, 226, 228, 229–230, 238, 239, 241, 250, 251–254, 262

Partner activities, 92, 130, 145, 155, 201

Prereading preparation, 20, 40, 108–109, 130–131, 150–151, 176–177, 197–198, 222, 246–247

Short-answer questions, 11, 13, 21, 30, 45–47, 69, 70, 77, 79, 88, 102, 113, 122, 136, 141–142, 143–144, 156–157, 158, 164–165, 166–167, 177, 182, 188, 190, 202, 203, 204, 211, 213, 228, 229, 236–237, 238, 239, 241, 252, 260, 262, 264

Skimming and scanning exercises, 5, 24, 43, 66–67, 91–92, 112, 134, 154–155, 179–180, 201, 226–227, 250

True/false questions, 4, 23, 42–43, 65–66, 90–91, 111, 133, 153, 179, 190, 200, 225–226, 249

Vocabulary in context, 118, 140–141, 163–164, 187, 210, 235–236, 259–260

Word search, 16, 34, 58, 83, 104, 124, 146, 171, 193, 216, 242, 267

Yes/no questions, 13

Graphs, 241

Lists, 15, 266

Prereading preparation, 2, 62–63, 88–89

Vocabulary in context, 10, 29, 52–53, 76, 98–99

SPEAKING

Group activities, 15

TOPICS

Alfred Nobel: A Man of Peace, 176–196

A Family Sees America Together, 2–19

A Healthy Diet for Everyone, 150–174

How Alike Are Identical Twins?, 40–61

How Earthquakes Occur, 246–270

Improving Lives with Pet Therapy, 130–149

Marie Curie: Nobel Prize Winner, 197–219

A New Way to Go, 108–126

Oil as an Important World Resource, 222–245

Robots: The Face of the Future, 88–107

The Search for Happiness through Adoption, 62–86

Volunteer Vacations, 20–37

VIEWING

Charts, 264

Illustrations, 222, 246

Maps, 15, 263

Photographs, 2, 21, 40, 88, 108, 150, 176, 197, 265

WRITING

Advertisements, 103

Answers to questions, 11, 13, 21, 30, 45–47, 53–54, 69, 70, 77, 79, 88, 99–100, 102, 108, 113, 119–120, 122, 131, 136, 141–142, 143–144, 150, 151, 156–157, 158, 164–165, 166–167, 177, 182, 188, 190, 202, 203, 204, 211, 213, 228, 229, 236–237, 238, 239, 241, 252, 260, 262, 264

Autobiographies, 214
Biographies, 15, 191, 214
Charts, 5, 24, 32, 44, 67, 92, 112, 122, 130, 131, 134, 150, 151, 155, 169, 180, 226, 247, 250
Compositions, 262
Description, 14, 33, 57, 82, 103, 122, 123, 144, 191, 211, 213, 239, 271
Diagrams, 20
Dialogues, 82
Diets/menus, 168–170, 171
Drawing, 123
Explanations, 33, 57, 79–80, 86, 103, 128, 144, 167, 211, 214, 220, 236, 260, 271
Group activities, 11, 20, 24, 30, 33, 53–54, 77, 99–100, 103, 119–120, 123, 144, 164–165, 168–169, 188, 191–192, 211, 236–237, 260
Instructions, 191
Journals, 14, 33, 57, 80, 102, 122, 144, 167, 191, 214, 239, 263
Letters, 144
Lists, 33, 57, 63, 88, 89, 123, 131, 167, 176, 222, 239, 240, 262, 271
Paragraphs, 14
Partner activities, 5, 33, 44, 57, 63, 67, 82, 108, 112, 130, 134, 150, 151, 155, 167, 176, 180, 222, 226, 240, 250, 271
Reporting, 20
Sentences, 201
Time lines, 201
Topics, 14, 33, 57, 79–80, 102, 122, 144, 167, 191, 214, 239, 262–263